GAME PLAN

The Definitive Playbook for
Starting or Growing Your Business

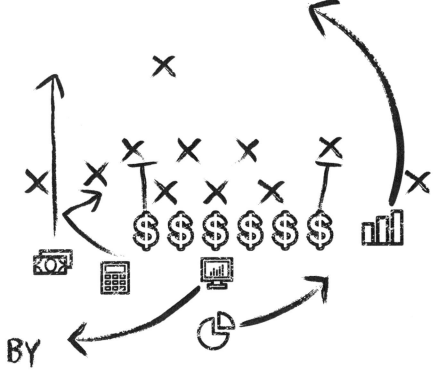

BY

WARREN BARHORST

WITH RUSTY BURSON

www.gameplanbook.com

AuthorHouse™
1663 Liberty Drive
Bloomington, IN 47403
www.authorhouse.com
Phone: 1-800-839-8640

First published by AuthorHouse 7/22/2010
First Edition, October 2008

Distributed by Renovo Partners, LLC

*For ordering information or special discounts for bulk purchases,
please contact Renovo Partners, LLC at 8220 Jones Road Suite
100 Houston, Texas 77065, (877) 7RENOVO or 281-677-9568.*

Library of Congress Cataloging-in-Publication Data
Barhorst, Warren E.
   *Game Plan: The definitive playbook for starting or growing your business/
   Warren E. Barhorst with Rusty Burson*
         p. ; cm.
*1. Entrepreneurship. 2. Starting a Business 3. Growing Your Business.
4. Success in Business. 5. Insurance Agents. 6. Insurance Sales.
I. Title. II. Title: The Definitive Playbook for Starting or Growing Your Business*

ISBN: 978-1-4520-4609-9 (sc)
ISBN: 978-1-4520-4610-5 (hc)
ISBN: 978-1-4520-4612-9 (e)

Library of Congress Control Number: 2010909266

Printed in the United States of America
Bloomington, Indiana

This book is printed on acid-free paper.

GAME PLAN

The Definitive Playbook for Starting or Growing Your Business

By Warren E. Barhorst with Rusty Burson

More detailed information about the topics covered in this book is available at:

www.gameplanbook.com.

The website is continually updated to provide the latest information, forms, instructions and tips to help you build or grow your business.

INTRODUCTION

What you have in your hands is not the typical, traditional, how-to business book. It's different in numerous ways from most business books that either bog you down with information overload or bore you to tears with textbook techniques.

There's a real strong chance that you will be highly entertained by reading this book. And more significantly, there's a real good chance that you will actually believe you are capable of starting or expanding your business. That's the primary goal of this book—to impart to you, the entrepreneur, a realistic, achievable approach to starting or expanding your business.

Because it's a different kind of business book, my advice is to read it differently than you have probably read most self-help or how-to business books in the past. I suggest you read this book from start to finish, take notes, highlight key points and spend some quiet time thinking and reflecting on what you have read. After you have completed reading the book, then leverage the website www. gameplanbook.com to begin your entrepreneurial journey. You can reference the book over and over again as you start or expand you business, but read it all the way through the first time.

The principles and examples in this book are all real. They are not intellectual theories from professors. This book is entirely based on a real individual sharing his real life experiences in going from a start-up operation to an above-average business, and then taking that solid business to a best-of-breed organization. I know it is real because I was there when "crazy dreams" were put on paper, committed to and ultimately realized. I was part of the "corporate team" receiving the crazy dream presentation. I remember thinking to myself, "If Warren can accomplish half of his business plan, we all win." Well, he has done it all...and more. We have won, and now you can win with his strategies, techniques, principles, etc.

As for me, I am now a retired insurance executive and a partner with Warren on several new business ventures. I am an ex-officio member of his virtual board, and more importantly, his friend.

Get yourself ready to think, to laugh, and to be challenged. To read this book properly you need a fresh highlighter, a new pad of paper, a few pens and an open mind.

Enjoy your entrepreneurial journey!

David K Hollingsworth
Managing Partner
Renovo Partners, LLC

DEDICATION

To Lisa, my wife and the MVP of my life. To my children, Spencer, Ashley and Shelby, who are undoubtedly can't-miss prospects for future stardom in whatever business fields they choose to pursue. To all of our Employees, Agents and Nationwide Insurance partners, the loyal teammates, all-stars and role players who have propelled us to phenomenal heights. – Warren Barhorst

To my mother, Vicki Pekurney, and my father, Russ Burson, who first encouraged me to dream big. And to Warren Barhorst, a true friend and terrific partner who inspired me and taught me with virtually every interview we did. – Rusty Burson

PREFACE

Let's get straight to the point right here on the first line of the first page of this book: You've got what it takes to succeed. There's no doubt in my mind about that. You are equipped to succeed in business. You have the genetic makeup to thrive as an entrepreneur. You have what it takes to make it on your own, to gain financial independence, to leave a legacy for your children. There it is, folks. There's your endorsement. There's your validation. There's the vote of confidence that so many people spend their entire working lives longing to hear.

I don't really care what your past experiences are; I don't care how many times you've tried and failed before; I don't care what your family members or previous employers have said to you; and I sure as hell don't care how that manipulative, conniving little inner voice may be trying to convince you otherwise. You've got what it takes. Period. End of discussion.

How do I know? Well, first of all, you probably wouldn't be holding this particular book in your hands if you were not motivated, educated and at least receptive to learning some of the necessary strategies and techniques to start your own business or expand it further. I fully realize that some lazy, dim-witted people also read books, but from what I've seen in bookstores and inside countless airplanes, most of them typically steer clear of anything that would encourage them to get off their butts and take the necessary action steps to dynamically shape their future. I've seen plenty of sappy, sultry and sorcery-based novels brought onto airplanes during my business travels, but most of the readers rarely stop in first-class.

I assure you that this is no *Harlequin* or *Harry Potter*, slouch-on-the-couch novel where you will be encouraged to "lose yourself"

ACHIEVE

in someone else's fantasy life. No, I believe you picked up this book to discover the best in yourself, to be challenged, to transform your business visions into bottom-line profits. If that's the case, you are already on the right track.

The second reason I believe you have what it takes has to do with your genetic makeup. I believe every man has been designed by his Creator with the ability to achieve the dreams that have been placed in his heart. This is not a Christian book, and I am not going to preach to you. But I am a God-fearing man, and I firmly

DREAMS ARE ILLUSTRATIONS...FROM THE BOOK YOUR SOUL IS WRITING ABOUT YOU.
- MARSHA NORMAN

believe that we have all been given the tools to accomplish great things (but it is up to us to sharpen those tools). Furthermore, I believe that man was created to be daring and passionate; to chase his dreams; to reflect the Creator's glory by conquering fears and taking risks; to run the race valiantly. In his book *Wild at Heart*, John Eldredge may have said it best: "Most men think they are simply here on earth to kill time—and it's killing them. But the truth is precisely the opposite. The secret longing of your heart, whether it's to build a boat and sail it, to write a symphony and

play it, to plant a field and care for it—those are the things you were made to do. That's what you're here for. Explore, build, conquer… but it's going to take risk, and danger, and there's the catch. Are we willing to live with the level of risk God invites us to? Something inside us hesitates."

Indeed, most men never reach the professional—or personal—level of success that they were designed to achieve because something inside them stops them in their tracks. It's the fear of the unknown,

the fear of failure, the fear of taking risks. And it's usually brought to our attention by that sappy little inner voice, telling us that "we can't" or that "we're not good enough" or that "we don't have what it takes." So, we hesitate. And if you hesitate long enough, you're done—defeated—demoralized.

As the poet George Herbert once wrote, "he begins to die, that quits his desires." Once you give up on your dreams—once you relegate yourself to your current circumstances you might as well purchase the casket and cemetery plot because you have stopped living and begun dying.

My dream was not to be an insurance agent. The insurance industry, with its residual income and unlimited profit potential, simply provided me with the vehicle to reach my dream destination: financial independence. Dating back to the time I first purchased my own bicycle, I've always wanted to be financially independent. Not because I possessed an insatiable love for money; not because I wanted to live in a mansion; not because I wanted to own a fleet of sports cars or yachts. My internal desire to be financially independent can easily be traced to my childhood. As the youngest

of six kids, I watched my father bust his butt throughout his entire professional career. He worked for a respected, nationally-known company for 42 years. Day after day, week after week, and year after year, my father devoted his working life to collecting a paycheck while helping someone else get ahead. My father, on the other hand, basically stayed on the corporate treadmill, sweating it out, but never really moving forward. He never made more than a very modest income, and he was continuously passed over for virtually every promotion that he could have possibly received. As a result, my mother also worked the cafeteria line at my elementary school to help make ends meet. With six kids in the house, the ends rarely met.

We weren't dirt poor, and we weren't left wondering where our next meal was coming from, either, although we knew it wasn't coming from an upscale restaurant. I am extremely proud of my parents because they devoted their lives to developing their children. My five siblings and I have a total of six undergraduate degrees, two master's degrees, one Ph.D., two M.D.s and a host of professional designations behind our names. My parents put their kids first, and we owe much of our success to them. But despite all of that, money was a constant source of concern for my parents, and I decided at a fairly young age that I wanted to do something professionally that would allow me to earn a comfortable living. I didn't want to fret about money every day. I didn't want to live in fear of the car breaking down. I didn't care if I shopped at Neiman Marcus, but I didn't want to be forced to shop at the Salvation Army Thrift Store. So, I went to college— first at Stephen F. Austin (SFA) in Nacogdoches, Texas—and later earned a degree in industrial distribution from Texas A&M University in College Station.

It may have been in college that I truly began to realize one of the most important lessons of my life: I've got what it takes to succeed. I'd like to tell you that I learned this by breezing through my classes. Of course, I'd also like to tell you that beautiful women have always been mesmerized by my rugged good looks. But both of those statements would be nothing more than bold-faced lies. The truth is that I wanted to quit college two or three times. But my father, who was told numerous times that he never earned the promotions he wanted because he didn't own a college degree, wouldn't allow me to quit. So, I continued to persevere through my classes, scratching and clawing to grasp the concepts that seemed to come easily to many of the smarter students that shared those classrooms with me.

I earned the degree that hangs on my office wall in 1988. But the more valuable lessons I learned in college had nothing to do with actually making grades. The most masterful sales job I've ever pulled off came in college. I noticed Lisa Highsmith shortly after I transferred from Stephen F. Austin to Texas A&M. Like most beautiful women I've encountered throughout my life, she initially wanted absolutely nothing to do with me. But after basically stalking her around campus for several months, she was left with two options: Go out with me or solicit a court-ordered restraining order. Fortunately, she chose to go out with me. She was out of my league in every sense, and I knew I was running a sizeable risk of being rejected. But despite what my inner voice was trying to tell me—like, "You don't have a chance"—I set my sights on winning Lisa's heart. With a little luck and a lot of begging, I did just that. Here's what I concluded from this courtship and here's the point of including this story in the book: If I could sell Lisa on spending the rest of her life with me, I figured I could sell just about anything else. In other words, "I've got what it takes."

An equally significant realization for me that occurred in college came on the football field. Let me first say that I was a fairly decent prep fullback and linebacker at Jersey Village High School in the Houston area. But I was certainly not big-time college football material. In fact, when I came out of high school I weighed about 180 pounds, and I had convinced myself that my football career had come to an end. Truthfully, I was scared to even give it a shot at Division I-AA Stephen F. Austin. I had spent much of my life dreaming about playing college football, and I'd spent countless hours envisioning myself at Texas A&M. I even had two older brothers and a sister who had preceded me at A&M. But fear stopped me in my tracks. In the pit of my stomach—although I never would have admitted it to anyone else—I didn't want to go to A&M because I wasn't sure I could cut it. And I didn't want to try out for the SFA football team because I didn't want to risk the chance of making a fool of myself or proving to myself that I didn't have what it took.

After two years at SFA, however, I had gained about 30 pounds and—more significantly—a little courage. At the urging of my older brother, Alan, who had returned to A&M to work on his Master's degree in mechanical engineering, I transferred to A&M and also decided to try out for the 12th Man Kickoff Team. That team, consisting of 10 walk-on players and one scholarship kicker, had gained tremendous national recognition under then-head coach Jackie Sherrill. Approximately 350 students tried out for it the same year I did. To make a long story short, I made the squad and found myself lining up against Notre Dame's Heisman Trophy winner Tim Brown in the 1988 Cotton Bowl in Dallas. Brown, who would go on to become the Oakland Raiders' all-time leading receiver, was one of the most gifted athletes I had ever seen. En route to winning the 1987 Heisman, he established a Notre Dame school record—which, at the time of this writing, still stands—for the most career kickoff return yards. Brown was from Dallas, and he had played high school ball against one of my teammates, defensive back Chet Brooks. Before the game, Brooks told the members of the 12th Man Kickoff Team that, if we had the opportunity, we should steal Brown's belt towel. "If you steal his towel, it will drive him crazy," Brooks told us.

6

Tim Brown   Me

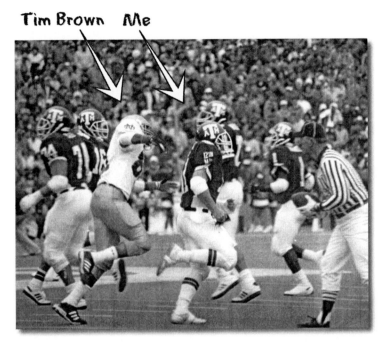

He was right. After we had taken a 28-10 lead in the fourth quarter, we kicked off to Notre Dame, and Brown was about two steps away from breaking my tackle and going the distance for a touchdown. But luckily, I managed to bring him down and then acted upon Brooks' suggestion. I ripped the towel from Brown's belt, bounced up and started running toward the A&M sideline. Before I made it to our bench, though, Brown jumped on my back, tackling me and grabbing his towel back. The infuriated Brown was flagged for a 15-yard unsportsmanlike conduct penalty and we went on to win the game, 35-10. On the following day, newspapers throughout the state of Texas and across the country featured pictures, headlines and stories with my name prominently in print. And years later, in a survey conducted by the Texas A&M Lettermen's Association, my thievery of Brown's towel was voted the fifth most memorable moment in Aggie sports history.

Here's the lesson to be learned from this story: Stealing someone else's ideas and then implementing those strategies on your own can propel you into the spotlight beyond your wildest imagination. I'm living proof of that. And not just in the sports arena. I've been doing the same thing in business for many years, as I initially built my insurance agency from the ground up. I've stolen more ideas from successful agents and entrepreneurs over the last 20 years than Rickey Henderson stole bases. Putting those ideas into action hasn't earned me the same amount of headlines I received when I swiped Tim Brown's towel. But those ideas have helped me build a business that, as I write today, is one of the largest hybrid exclusive insurance agencies in the country. The success we have achieved in the insurance industry has also enabled me to expand into other ventures such as real estate development, business consulting, insurance wholesaling and motivational speaking.

That leads me to the final reason I am firmly convinced that you have what it takes to thrive as an entrepreneur: If a knucklehead like me—an extraordinarily ordinary guy if ever there was one—can build a multi-faceted enterprise like the one I now own, then I know you can build something big, as well. The ensuing chapters include years of my own experiences, input, analysis and strategies. We hope to entertain you, encourage you, motivate you, stimulate your imagination and spur you on toward accomplishing your dreams. This is not your typical business book. For one, it won't put you to sleep. More significantly, it will provide you with the foundation to build your business. This book supplies a high-level view of proven universal business fundamentals. When you decide to act upon these principles, the nuts and bolts of all the concepts and specific examples are found at www.gameplanbook.com.

Some of the ideas in this book will be simple to implement; others may cause you to stretch and to expand outside your comfort zone. And, from time to time, I'm sure that your own little inner voice will be trying to convince you that you could never do this or that.

Don't believe it. You've got what it takes to succeed. I know it, and by the time you are finished with this book, I'm confident that you will be able to prove it to the most important person of all: yourself.

So, steal my ideas; overcome your own fears; and prepare to tackle any obstacles that may come your way. From personal experience, I can tell you that even a Heisman Trophy winner can be brought down, as long as you truly convince yourself that you've got what it takes.

Dreams are illustrations... from the book your soul is writing about you. – Marsha Norman

Some of the world's greatest feats were accomplished by people not smart enough to know they were impossible. – Doug Larson

It's never too late to be who you might have been. – George Eliot

God gives us dreams a size too big so that we can grow into them. – Author Unknown

CHAPTER I

HOLD ON TO YOUR DREAMS

Depending on how old you are and what your musical preferences may be, you may recall the three-man Canadian rock band Triumph, which formed in 1975 and gained fairly widespread popularity in the United States in the late 1970s and early '80s. The band featured a unique brand of melodic hard rock, and, for whatever reason, it received some of its most extensive airplay in Texas during my teen-age years. Fortunately for you, I am writing this book and until we come out with an audio version, you will not be required to listen to me sing my renditions of some of my favorite Triumph tunes. Like the band's name suggests, Triumph

was at its best when it was singing about what it took to be successful. You could apply the lyrics from *Fight the Good Fight* or *Lay It On the Line* to just about any endeavor you are undertaking. But the song that was particularly poignant to me was *Hold On* from the band's third album, *Just a Game*. I'm not sure what the exact inspiration was for the song, but I do know that these lyrics have provided some introspective moments through the years: "listen to your heart and hold on to your dreams."

Maybe Socrates, Aristotle or Ralph Waldo Emerson uttered wiser words about perseverance, but that trio couldn't have sung it better than Triumph. If you want to be successful in practically any business endeavor, you'd better be prepared to hold on to your dreams. If you don't, I can practically guarantee you that someone—or some set of adverse circumstances—will snatch them away from you.

I cannot possibly predict how long or winding your road to financial independence will be if you choose to start your own business or if you have decided to dramatically grow your business. But I promise you that it will not happen overnight, and it will probably be filled with numerous potholes, roadblocks, discouraging detours and hazardous conditions. It won't necessarily be a scenic journey, either. Along the way, your path will likely be littered with the road-kill and wreckage of those who abandoned their dreams and lost their drive. I've seen it a thousand times before. Plenty of well-meaning, hard-charging people have started off blazing a course to financial freedom in business, but after a couple of wrong turns or blown tires, they lose their sense of direction and purpose. Some pull over to rest; others are lost forever in a traffic jam that never seems to move forward; and others simply turn around and head in a different direction. Very few ever seem to push forward through the congestion. Fewer seem to have the ability to shift into another gear to distance themselves from the perpetual rat race.

So, what separates the run-of-the-mill businesses from the extraordinary ones? What propels a handful of entrepreneurs to annual income levels that much of the population won't make in a lifetime?

A number of different factors figure into the equation, and we will spend the rest of this book discussing them. I am firmly convinced, however, that the very first thing you need to do—before you make your first contact and before you even begin to contemplate a location, a service, a product or anything else—is to dream. In fact, I would go so far as to say that if you don't spend an ample amount of time dreaming now, then you will probably spend far too much time wishing and working during what should be your retirement years. Dreams are that important.

I suspect some of you analytical types are probably tempted to shut the book right now, skip forward to the nuts-and-bolts material in ensuing chapters or simply write me off as some pie-in-the-sky daydreamer who possibly spent too much time trippin' while listening to Triumph. But hear me out. If you only act on one principle in this entire book, this is the one to wrap your arms around. It's basic; it's rudimentary; and it's probably something that you have heard many times before. But it is literally one of the fundamental keys for taking your "game" from weekend hacker status to PGA-level. It can propel your budget allowances from crumbs to caviar, and it can transform your business from striving to thriving.

I've spent many years studying some of the most successful entrepreneurs and business models in the country. I've watched

DREAMING

them from afar; I've quizzed entrepreneurs and employees over lunch; I've analyzed their techniques, their strategies, their offices, their day-to-day routines, their wardrobes and practically everything else. Beyond that, I've read enough self-help, motivational and entrepreneurial books to start my own library. And in attending success/sales/motivational seminars and conferences, along with industry-specific functions, through the years, I've probably seen more hotel ballrooms than some wedding planners. But if I had to narrow the underlining theme of all of these books, private discussions and mass motivational meetings down to one principle, it would be this: Never underestimate the power of your own dreams.

From personal experience; however, I would take this message two steps further and say: Never underestimate the power of holding on to your own dreams and walking toward them. That may sound like a subtle difference, but it actually makes all the difference in the world. Holding on to your dreams and making them real takes some time and effort; it requires some planning and nurturing; and it is something that very few people in any profession understand. The facts back up that assertion in an alarming way.

For example, according to the United States Department of Labor's Bureau of Statistics, approximately 2.7 million youths graduated from American high schools between October 2004 and October 2005. If you surveyed those students, I'm sure you would find that the vast majority of them had big, glorious dreams about their financial/professional future. In fact, a whopping 68.6 percent (1.8 million) of those high school graduates were attending colleges or universities in

2005, providing further evidence that the majority of these youths are serious about their financial future.

On the other hand, according to a 2005 study conducted by leading academic scholars from 10 universities and five business experts in personal finance, approximately 30 million workers in America today—one in four—are seriously financially distressed with their personal financial situation. The author of this particular report, E. Thomas Garman, professor emeritus at Virginia Tech, went on to say that many of these 30 million American workers "do not even have hope that they will one day catch up financially." Furthermore, according to Steve Rhode, the president of Myvesta, a nonprofit financial health center, "half of Americans are currently struggling to control excessive spending and debt." And finally, according to the U.S. Department of Commerce, only five percent of all Americans are financially independent at age 65. The same DOC study indicated that 75 percent of all retirees are forced to depend on Social Security and/or family and friends as their only sources of income.

So, based on those studies, here are the sobering conclusions we can draw from what those 2.7 million high school graduates from the class of 2005 have to look forward to: 675,000 will eventually become seriously distressed about their financial future; 1.35 million will struggle with excessive spending and debt; and only 135,000 will reach the age of 65 financially independent. Or, put another way, more than 2.5 million of today's 2.7 million high

school graduates will eventually be relying on Social Security—if it still exists—or family and friends to supply the basic necessities of life. Sobering, isn't it? And remember, we're talking about the high school graduates here. Toss in the dropouts, and the numbers become even gloomier.

What happens to all those dreams of youth? Why do so few realize their financial potential? Why do 95 percent of Americans reach retirement age without financial peace of mind?

Every case is obviously unique, with its own set of circumstances. But I am convinced that the vast majority of people simply lose sight of their dreams. No one ever comes out of high school or college planning to live from paycheck to paycheck. No one ever enters the workforce with plans of declaring bankruptcy, running up huge amounts of debt, being passed over for promotions or watching the years rush by with little to show for them. Likewise, in the insurance industry, I don't know of many agents who enter into the industry hoping to be on the constant agency treadmill where he/she is always between 1,500 and 2,500 policies in force with little—or no—growth. But it happens all the time. I regularly talk to agents who are absolutely miserable about their current circumstance and their future prospects because they can't ever seem to get beyond that 1,500 to 2,500 level. They entered the industry with big plans, but they inevitably become lost in the service work created by those existing policies. Your existing clients throw new problems at you; you manage to find time to replace the 10 percent of the clients who leave you annually for another provider; and you wake up one day—after a few years or, in some cases, after a few decades—with the realization that you are nothing more than a glorified customer service representative. You can't ever really get ahead because you spend all your time talking to, and attempting to retain, your existing clients. Sound familiar? If you are in the insurance industry, I bet it does.

Generally speaking, after a few years on the job most people tend to settle in. I'm not referring to settling down, as when you are done sewing your wild oats. No, this has nothing to do with finding a spouse and no longer spending too much time on a bar stool. I'm talking about settling in to their current circumstances and letting go of their dreams. They begin to settle for the rut; they begin to settle for the four percent raises from their company; they begin to settle for a certain tax bracket and neighborhood; and they begin to downgrade their dreams. Or worse, they lose sight of them altogether.

That's why it is so important to hold on to your dreams. Virtually everybody starts out with them, but the daily grind—mortgage payments, car payments, family living expenses, healthcare costs, time constraints, business disappointments, family issues, stress, etc.—begin to slowly wash those dreams out of the consciousness. Think about your own childhood for a moment.

What was your dream as a kid? Maybe it was to be a professional baseball player. Perhaps it was to be a famous actor or singer. Possibly it was to become president... of a company or of the United States. What happened to those  dreams? When did you allow them to die? When did you convince yourself that they were silly? Was it when you went 0-for-4 at the plate in the biggest game of the season? Was it when your coach told you that you were too slow? Was it when you were benched in favor of the kid with more talent? Maybe your friends or father said you weren't tough enough. Maybe you began convincing yourself that professional baseball was out of reach, after all. Whatever the case, slowly, over time, most kids begin to lose sight of their dreams.

The same thing happens to us as adults, as we allow self-doubts to replace our dreams. We settle for a small sliver of the pie; we lose confidence in ourselves with every rejection; we focus on the bug guts on our own windshield instead of the road ahead. In virtually every walk of life I've seen that those who don't hold on to their dreams will eventually work for—or report to—those who do.

So, here's my challenge to you: Don't just dream; hold on to your dreams and focus your actions toward achieving them. Visualize them. Make them have feeling. The very best  way to start is by writing them down. Ever since I was a kid, I have been a big believer in writing down your dreams and goals and then revisiting them regularly. In fact, the person who first truly convinced me about the power of writing down my dreams and goals was a woman named Pat Lockett-Smith, who was my teacher in a high school study skills class. She made a profound impact on my development that I have never forgotten, and today, she happens to be one of my clients. How's that for applying what you learn?

Pat helped me to refine my goal-setting skills, but it was something I had been doing for years. In fact, not too long ago, I was reminded about the power of writing down your dreams and goals when I came across a sheet of paper that I had written as an adolescent. My parents lived in the same house for about 30 years, and my mother saved practically everything. She's a pack rat in every sense; the kind of person who will purchase new furniture, but won't part with the old furniture for sentimental reasons. When she was finally forced to clean out the house a few years back, however, she filled up four or five boxes with my stuff from school. As my son Spencer and I went through the boxes to determine if

there was anything worth keeping, we found report cards from my grade school days, drawings from kindergarten, etc. We were laughing and giggling at what we found, and we came across a goal-setting sheet I did in the seventh grade. I had written down these things that I wanted:

- A big house
- A good-looking girlfriend
- An AC-Cobra (sports car)
- More patience

After reading the list, my son fell on the floor because he was laughing so hard. He then looked at me, smiled and said, "Dad, you've got everything you wanted except for more patience." In addition to paying a wonderful compliment to his mother—my "hot" girlfriend-turned-wife—and slamming me about my occasional lack of patience, Spencer quickly realized the power of writing down your goals. At the time, I had an AC Cobra sitting in the garage of my dream house. And inside that house was the woman of my dreams. I'm still working on that "more patience" issue—and I may for the rest of my life. But I was really taken aback by the awesome power of writing down your dreams and goals. I had no idea at the time I wrote those things down how I was going to attain those things. But I truly believe that when you take the time to write down your goals, your subconscious will find a way to fulfill the image your mind is painting.

So, what are you waiting for? If you haven't already done so, write down your dreams and goals. Do it now. Pull out a notepad, open up the laptop, or e-mail yourself on your PDA. It doesn't have to be anything elaborate; it doesn't have to be well-written or entertaining; it doesn't even have to make sense to anyone

19

but you. It just has to be written down for it to ever become real.

Okay, if you actually took the time to stop reading and jot down your goals, you are now part of an elite sector of society. (If not, do it now). In the course of attending those various seminars I mentioned previously, I was rather astonished to learn that only about five percent of the population actually takes the time to write down their goals. Interesting number, huh? Let's see: Five percent of the population writes down their dreams and goals and five percent of Americans reach their retirement age financially independent. Coincidence?

I think not. Writing down your dreams and goals is a paramount step toward achieving them. Then, regularly revisiting them—no matter how lofty they may seem today—makes those dreams and goals seem far more attainable than impossible. And by "regularly revisiting them," I'm not referring to when you're cleaning out your desk drawers or—in my case—when your mother finally cleans out her attic. This should not be an annual thing, either, as so many do when they make New Year's resolutions. Not even monthly. I'm talking about going over them weekly or even putting them in a place where you will at least see them daily. I am referring to cutting out pictures of your dream house, your new storefront, your ideal vehicle or your fantasy vacation destination and putting them on the

refrigerator or your mirror. This will help you visualize your dreams and then keep those visions in front of you. Seeing these dreams and goals keeps you focused; reading them regularly keeps you on track toward reaching them; and it greatly increases your resolve to handle the obstacles and objections that will inevitably come your way. By firmly determining what you want, you will figure out what you must give up—sleep, time, effort—in order to get it.

The entire writing/reviewing process takes very little time, but it  forces you to visualize your goals; it creates a commitment on your part; and it serves as your roadmap to success. Perhaps most important, that simple act prevents you from settling, compromising or completely losing sight of your dreams. You WILL NOT be derailed by a few rejections, financial hard times, frustrations or any other series of disappointments if you keep your dreams in front of you. On the contrary, your subconscious will help you find a way to make happen what is constantly in front of you.

How did Michael Jordan become the greatest basketball player in the history of the NBA even after he failed to make the varsity

> If we take the time to dream; if we are specific in the visualization of our definition of success; and if we write our goals and dreams down on paper, our odds of individual success go up by a rate of about 95 percent.

on his initial tryout? He kept his dreams in front of him. How did Wilma Rudolph, one of the greatest American sprinters of all time, win three Olympic gold medals after being paralyzed—the result of double pneumonia and scarlet fever—when she was 4 years old? Her dreams were bigger than her obstacles. How did Jim Carrey, who was forced to quit school because of his family's severe economic troubles, become one of the greatest comedic actors of our time, even though he never received his high school diploma? He wrote himself a seven-figure check and kept it in his wallet to remind himself of what he wanted to attain through acting.

There are literally thousands of examples of well-known men and women who achieved their dreams by refusing to give in to negative circumstances around them. For example:

• Lucille Ball became one of the most famous and beloved American actresses of all time. But she was initially told, in 1927, by the head instructor of the John Murray Anderson Drama School to "find another profession. Any other (profession)."

• Louis L'Amour, the great western novelist who died in 1988, wrote more than 100 novels in his lifetime and sold more than 225 million copies. But he also received approximately 350 rejections before making his first sale.

Now, that is true perseverance. I'm not actually certain if Louis L'Amour wrote down his goals or if Wilma Rudolph held onto her dreams by visiting them on a regular basis. But I am convinced, as Zig Ziglar once wrote, that "the mind completes whatever picture we put in it."

I've already provided you the facts to prove it. So, allow me to beat a dead horse once again. Write down your financial goals; picture what the house you want to eventually buy looks like; estimate the exact amount of income you need to become stress-free in terms of your financial peace of mind. And then constantly review your list and update it.

Of course, the same principles that apply to your personal goals also are applicable to your organization. I am thoroughly convinced that your agency, your company, your organization, etc. will not reach its full potential without a business plan. Before I elaborate any further on the importance of a business plan, however, please allow me—for the sake of example—to escort you down my own Memory Lane. I promise it will be a relatively short trip, but it may help you see how to stretch your visions as you grow your business.

When I started out in the insurance business with my wife, Lisa, our goals were actually rather moderate. Lisa and I were married in college, and we had our first child in 1987 while I was still in school. So, we truly knew the meaning of "lean financial times." In fact, shortly after I graduated from A&M, an artist named Rick Rush came out with a limited-edition painting called *Lead by the Spirit: Cotton Bowl 1988*" that featured me prominently. It was an artistic tribute to Texas A&M's 12th Man Kickoff Team, and it featured several 12th Man Kickoff Team members tackling Tim Brown. The artist's rendition included a prominent picture of me, featuring my name on the back of the jersey. I was in the office of former A&M head coach Jackie Sherrill one day after the painting was released, and he asked me if I had seen it. I called the artist and was informed that I could purchase a print for $500. I think my initial response was, "Yeah, right." We barely had enough money to purchase diapers, let alone paintings. Fortunately, my sister Eileen loaned me the money to buy the painting, but it took a considerable amount of time to pay it back to her.

In other words, we certainly weren't coming from money. And my initial visions were not as big as they should have been. When I started out in the insurance industry, my goal was simply to get to a point where we were grossing $20,000 of revenue per month. At that point in my life, I had just left the corporate world, and I was bound and determined to make it on my own. As I mentioned in the Preface of this book, I spent much of my youth watching my father get passed over for promotions because he didn't have a college degree. So, I went to college, earned my degree and figured that I would soon be on the fast track to success because I had that degree in hand. Of course, I also figured that my beloved Texas A&M Aggies were on the cusp of a football national championship.

I was wrong on both accounts (although I will never completely lose hope on the Aggies). I took my degree in industrial distribution and I went to work for a company called Mannesmann DEMAG as an assistant to a district manager. I was told it would take eight to twelve months for me to be trained to become a district manager. After busting my butt for about three months, I was ready. I had written down my goals, reorganized the office and created libraries of competitive information because I wanted to be out talking to people in the field and selling products. I was motivated, and I was a machine when it came to selling overhead bridge cranes, hoists and big capital equipment. About six months into that job, I was given a territory (New Mexico and North Texas) a little ahead of schedule. In a short amount of time, my territory grew to include seven states and seventy distributorships. By all accounts, I was on the fast track to success. Even my evaluations were, for the most part, nothing short of glowing.

For all I was doing for the company, though, I quickly learned a lesson about working for someone else. Along with all the radiant remarks in my performance reviews, also came comments like, "Warren is intolerant of other people's inability to get their job done."

Your damn right I was! (Remember my patience issues). I wanted to push the envelope; I wanted to move and shake; and I wanted everyone around me to have the same level of passion and commitment as I possessed. It didn't take me long to realize that would never happen as long as I was working for someone else. I took the lousy four percent raises for a while, but I became totally frustrated with the corporate bureaucracy. I was working twice as hard—and probably three times as effectively—as the 54-year-old salesmen in our organization. But because I was 24, I was making considerably less. That eventually drove me to find a way where I could work for myself and to find a profession where I could make what I deserved.

So, as Lisa and I ventured off into business for ourselves in 1993, we determined that the magic revenue number for us was $20,000 per month. That would give us roughly $10,000 a month to pay for the operating expenses of the office and $10,000 a month to keep for ourselves. At the time, I thought an income of $120,000 per year would have us set for life. (I encourage you to dream much bigger, especially in terms of today's economy). But I took that dream dollar amount and wrote it down at the top of a sheet of paper. Then, I began to write down underneath it what I would need to do to reach that level of income. For example, I knew I needed an office location; I knew I needed computers, software, telephones and other office necessities, as well. Pretty soon, I had a rough budget outline. Then, taking that same approach to employees, I began to develop an organizational chart.

Keep in mind that I didn't have any employees at that point. Nor did I have the money to hire a fleet of employees. It was only Lisa and me. But as I have said repeatedly, you have to dream it and visualize it before you can achieve it. I dreamed of the organization that I would eventually like to have, which included an office manager, a CFO, a marketing director, etc. Initially, Lisa or I handled all of those tasks, but simply developing that organizational chart kept me focused on what I needed to do, along with how much income I needed to generate, in order to fill those slots and fulfill the visions I had in mind. Admittedly, my initial organizational chart changed and evolved over the years as much as my goals and ambitions did. But it was very important to me to have a plan right from the start, and it allowed me to hire—and fire—people who did or did not buy into my visions for success. (I'll elaborate on hiring principles and practices, along with some of my own mistakes, in much greater detail in ensuing chapters). The point here is that long before I actually hired a marketing person or anyone else, I had a vision of what my organization would look like and, most significantly, I had it on paper.

The most important business preparation I did, however, was writing a business plan right from the start. I won't beat this into the ground like I did with the importance of writing down your personal goals, but let me emphasize that it is extremely important to the overall direction of your business. Nobody in their right mind would go on a long journey, especially into unfamiliar territory, without reviewing a map and charting a course. No one would allow an architect to build a dream house or an office building without first developing blueprints. Yet, highly educated, motivated people dive into business for themselves all the time with no road map for success.

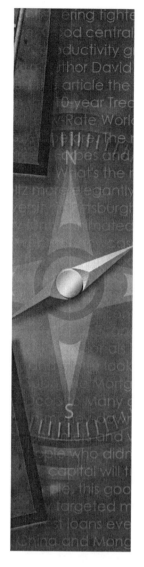

It's not that difficult to create a business plan. Simply go to our website at **www.gameplanbook.com** to view some samples, do an Internet search for the words "business plan" or go into a software program such as Power Point, or Excel where a template exists that asks you questions. All you have to do is answer them, and when you're done, you have a rough business plan. You can also access the United States Small Business Administration's website (www.sba.gov), where you will find plenty of tips and examples of business plans from a variety of industries. Don't drag your feet in writing this initial plan. The first business plan you write will undoubtedly change. I practically guarantee it. In fact, in the next chapter we will cover some of the comprehensive issues you must address if you are going to use your business plan to gain outside funding. But no matter what, your business plan—along with your vision—will grow over time. Your mind will start thinking, wondering, expanding.

In 2002, I wrote a $50 million business plan for Nationwide Insurance, and I invited the corporate executives to my Houston office to hear my presentation and to make it publicly known. The plan I wrote contained about 200 pages. In comparison, the first one I ever wrote—the one that was designed to help me generate $20,000 per month—was no more than two to three pages. It may have been brief, but it also set the foundation for everything my wife and I, along with our organization, have accomplished.

Today, all of my managing agents are required to create their own business plans. We discuss the plans; we make changes and edits; and I force them to stretch their goals. It's no different than when I played sports and my coach sat down with me and went over my goals. Writing those things down and making them public drives you to make them come true. Nowadays, even when I'm on a

Business Plan

Marketing

Market Analysis

Ideas

Brainstorming

Testing

Finished Product

Clients

Services

Sales

Profit

Payments

Earnings

Transaction

Delivery

Feedback

diet I tell people about my weight-loss goals because it holds me accountable. If I'm talking to somebody that I just met, and we're talking about business, I might tell them that I have thirty insurance offices and we're adding five more locations this year. It would be easy for me to say that we simply have thirty offices, but writing my goals down, reviewing them and making them public keeps me energized and focused on that goal.

We're not talking brain surgery or rocket science here; it's just common sense. But far too few people ever capitalize on the amazing power of visualization. Resolve to take five minutes to write down your goals, and you just may find yourself in the five percent of Americans who retire with no financial worries. Before we move on to the nuts and bolts of business, I want to leave you with one more story about the power of visualization. The full story appeared in the book, *A 2nd Helping of Chicken Soup for the Soul,* and it truly depicts the amazing power we all possess if we would just tap into it. Here's the shortened version:

Major James Nesmeth was an avid, but average golfer, consistently shooting in the mid 90s. But Nesmeth dreamed about dramatically improving his golf game, and for seven years he did nothing but visualize his game. He never practiced his swing; he never pulled out his putter; he never even watched any golf on TV. He simply visualized his game improving. At the end of that seven-year stretch, Nesmeth cut 20 strokes off his average, shooting a personal-best 74 the first time he stepped back onto the course.

How'd he do it? Well, Nesmeth didn't have much of a choice. He spent those seven years as a prisoner of war in North Vietnam, surviving in solitude in a cage that was approximately four and one-half feet high and five feet long. During the first few months, he hoped and prayed for his release. Then he realized he had to find some way to occupy his mind or he would lose his sanity and probably his life. That's when he discovered the power of visualization. In his mind, Nesmeth selected his favorite golf course and started playing golf. Every day, he played a full 18 holes at the course, experiencing everything to the last detail. He pictured the weather conditions, the grass, the hazards, his playing partners, what he was wearing. He felt the grip of the club in his hands, while playing every shot and watching every roll of the ball. The visualization kept him alive, and when he finally was released, Nesmeth went out and shot a 74.

Now, think about what you can do if you will just take the time to write down your goals and hold onto your dreams. You don't need to spend seven years in a prison camp to shape your future. Simply devote some time toward developing your dreams, writing out a business plan and seeing yourself succeed. Remember the words of Triumph, and you will stop singing the blues.

GAME DAY PREP

1. Before starting a business or expanding one, the very first thing you need to do is:
   A. Borrow a boatload of money.
   B. Treat yourself to a two-week cruise with the profits you have not yet earned.
   C. Dream big.
   D. Forget it all together and join the rest of the rat race that never takes a chance and never experiences financial independence.

   Answer here_____

2. Five percent of Americans:
   A. Write down their goals.
   B. Revisit and revise their goals on a regular basis.
   C. Retire financially independent.
   D. All of the above.

   Answer here_____

3. The first business plan you write for your organization should:
   A. Be written in stone so that it never changes or grows.
   B. Be kept in a vault, where no one but you ever sees it.
   C. Be complex and filled with legal jargon so that you do not even fully comprehend what it means.
   D. Be revisited often, communicated, basic and straightforward.

   Answer here_____

More detailed information about the topics covered in this chapter is available at www.gameplanbook.com.

The website is continually updated to provide the latest information, forms, instructions and tips to help you build or grow your business.

Extra Points - Notes

Birds have bills too, and they keep on
singing. - Author Unknown

Tomorrow is the only day in the year
that appeals to a lazy man. - Jimmy Lyons

Procrastination is opportunity's
assassin. - Victor Kiam

CHAPTER 2
$ BUSINESS FUNDING
JUST DO IT

Watching an old movie can occasionally take you back in time. So can the lyrics of a song you haven't heard in ages. Even the scent of a particular perfume or cologne can bring back nostalgic memories of another time in your life. I bet I can take you back some 10 to 20 years with just three words: Just Do It.

Those simple, but magical marketing words literally swept the nation in the late 1980s and early '90s, becoming part of the American lexicon and transforming a sagging company into the undisputed king of the fitness world. You know the company; you know the indelible "Swoosh" stripe; and you know the glorious, sweat-soaked images that come to mind when that enduring slogan is uttered. Bo Jackson pounding a baseball into oblivion and bull-dozing Brian Bosworth into another zip code; John McEnroe pulverizing a tennis ball and shocking the tea-and-crumpets crowd at Wimbledon with his brash behavior and in-your-face intensity; Michael Jordan soaring gracefully through the air en route to 10 scoring titles and six NBA championships. The images were so powerful and clear: Just lace up your Nikes and take on the world. Just conquer your fears. Just get in the game. Just take the chance. Just fulfill your dreams of getting in shape.

Americans obviously embraced the message. Prior to the "Just Do It," advertising campaign, Reebok was winning—by a considerable margin—the athletic footwear fight in the United States. But following the 1988 unveiling of its "Just Do It" campaign, Nike, according to a mini case study written by the Center for Applied Research, increased its share of the domestic sport-shoe business from 18 percent in '88 to 43 percent in '98. During that same 10-year period, Nike's worldwide sales skyrocketed from $877 million to $9.2 billion.

Those numbers would seem to imply that Americans became fascinated by fitness; that our society, as a whole, finally became more focused on developing a hard body than sitting on a soft couch. From coast-to-coast, Americans were purchasing Nike merchandise and, apparently, buying into the "Just Do It" mentality. Based on Nike's sales alone, you might have been led to believe that our country was getting off its collective butt and onto its feet; that we were motivated to put down the remote control and take control of our physiques.

You, of course, should know differently. Look around the typical office setting. Spend a few moments people-watching at the mall.

Check out any downtown sidewalk around lunchtime. You'll likely discover more "wide loads" on the sidewalks than on the freeways. According to the American Obesity Association website (www.obesity.org), the percentage of overweight Americans has steadily increased since 1988. And now, some two decades after the "Just Do It" phenomenon became part of our culture, it is estimated that a whopping 64.5 percent of American adults are overweight.

That's nearly two-thirds of us. And nearly one-third of the adult population in the United States, age 20 years and older, is not just overweight, but is also considered to be obese.

Translation: As a society, we are not just doing it. In the mini case study written by the Center for Applied Research, it was estimated that 80 percent of the Nike athletic shoes that are sold annually in the U.S. are never used for the activities for which they were designed. The shoes may have been designed for running, but most of them end up on sedentary feet. Despite the fact that Nike has become one of the most recognizable and powerful symbols in American athletics/fitness, most consumers are obviously wearing them to run errands in their cars, not to run marathons.

As I am writing this, it is early January—one week after New Year's Day and two weeks removed from Christmas. I can't help but wonder how many fitness-related New Year's resolutions have already gone by the wayside and how many fitness-related gifts that were received on Christmas morning have already begun collecting dust.

So many Americans annually plan to take control of their physical condition. Many also take some of the necessary first steps, visualizing a healthier body and purchasing some exercise equipment. But most of us simply fail to follow through. We don't just do it; we just delay it. Fear of pain, fear of commitment and fear of failure cause many of us to hesitate. We put it off for a couple of days. Then for a couple of weeks. Eventually, we put it off long enough that the vision we may have had for a brand new, lean and improved body is forgotten altogether. At least until the following New Year's Eve, when the cycle starts all over again.

That's the way it goes for so many Americans regarding their physical fitness. Ditto for their fiscal fitness. How many Americans have spent at least some amount of time dreaming about opening their own business? How many Americans have pondered what it would be like to be financially independent? How many have purchased self-help books and business publications like this one to help kick-start their careers? How many have visualized a better financial life?

I don't have specific data to support this assumption, but my guess would be that practically everyone—from the poverty line to the

penthouse tenants in Manhattan—has spent at least some time dreaming about improving his or her monetary lot in life and easing their financial burdens. Yet, according to the 2005 U.S. Census Bureau, only 15 percent of the approximate 113 million households in America had an annual income of more than $100,000 per year. The 2005 numbers also revealed that only about 2 percent of American households earned more than $200,000 per year. The U.S. Census Bureau economic survey also revealed that households in the top two income quintiles—those with an annual household income exceeding $55,331—had a mean of two income earners, meaning that both Mom and Dad were busting their butts to make ends meet. Meanwhile, the real median income of households in the United States in 2005 was $46,326.

There are many socio-economic, demographic, health-related and educational reasons that 98 percent of the U.S. population doesn't gross $200,000 per year and that 85 percent of all American households fall short of six-figure incomes—even combined household incomes. I'm aware that some folks are doing the very best they can. I also know that there are some sad cases out there, while others are downright heartbreaking, especially when it involves circumstances beyond their control. So, I'm not naïve enough to believe that those numbers will ever dramatically change. But I do believe, beyond any doubt, that far more Americans are quite capable of making considerably more than they currently do.

Here, I'm talking to you. I started off this book by telling you that you have what it takes to be successful. You must believe that. And I spent the entire last chapter hammering you about the importance of dreaming and writing down your goals. In order to be successful in the insurance industry or any other, you must believe in yourself, and you will most certainly benefit from having clearly defined goals that keep you on track.

Those are the initial steps toward achieving peak fiscal fitness. The fact that you have already read this far also indicates that you are serious about taking control of your financial future. Many business books sold today end up on a shelf without ever being read. And many other well-meaning Americans glance through a book like this, nodding occasionally but never taking the necessary action steps to make a difference in their own lives.

So, let me pat you on the back for getting this far. But let me also paraphrase that famous slogan from Nike regarding what you should do with the information here: Get off your butt and just go do it.

Comparatively speaking, your purchase of this book is essentially, from a fiscal standpoint, the same as buying a pair of Nike running shoes designed to improve your physical condition. And now that you have read this far, you have basically begun to chart a course that can reshape your financial life. In essence, you've laced up your shoes, received a pep talk from a personal trainer and—if you followed through on your Chapter 1 instructions—you have your goals written down to guide you toward your dream destination.

Now, step into the gym. It's time to set the alarm clock and to commit to getting out of bed early and hitting the pavement while so many of your neighbors and colleagues are still sleeping. But understand that as soon as you commit to this cause—or practically any other—obstacles, excuses and self-doubt will creep into your mind. Commit to two weeks of running every day and see what happens. Unexpected thunderstorms will arrive; extreme cold fronts or unusually hot temperatures will sweep across your region; you'll come down with the flu; you may twist an ankle; and you're going to find other reasons to stay in bed. But get up and just do it. What you will discover is that running in the rain will not only strengthen your heart, it will also reinforce your resolve. Running against the wind is far more beneficial to your long-term conditioning than running with the wind at your back. And a bad run is far, far better than no run at all.

The same concepts apply to starting or further developing your business strategies. If you commit to following the principles and instructions in this book, obstacles will arise. Count on them. Finances may become stretched; time restraints may be increased; and your inner voice will undoubtedly provide you with hundreds of reasons why you shouldn't do it. You will likely be tempted to put it off until your current circumstances are better. But please remember this: While there are a million ways to waste today, there is not even one single way to get it back. Now is the time to take action, to create momentum, to create a sense of urgency and to take control of your financial future.

So, let's get to work by first eliminating some of the excuses that are bound to arise in your own mind. If you will hear me out, we can silence that sappy, self-doubting inner voice that sabotages most of the population. If you will act daily and diligently on the principles I am outlining, the voice you will begin to hear will be one of determination, not disbelief. There is no point in delaying it another day. Candidly, tomorrow is one day closer to your death than today. And as Henry Clay once said, "The time will come when winter (the end of your life) will ask you what you were doing all summer."

BUSTING THROUGH EXCUSE NO. 1 - MONEY

One of the business world's oldest clichés is that it takes money to make money. There's certainly some truth in that line of thinking, especially in terms of making really big money. But far too many people write off their dreams simply because they can't write a big check.

A lack of money is probably the No. 1 objection most people have when it comes to starting their own business or growing their existing operation. It often sounds like a justifiable reason for remaining in their current rut. In reality, though, it's probably more of an excuse than a legitimate reason. It certainly is in the insurance industry.

People ask me regularly: How much do I need to start my own agency? Then, they typically brace themselves, anticipating that I am about to give them an outlandish number that they could only produce with a winning lottery ticket. My answer often results in some shocked faces, but not because the figure is too high. I'm convinced that a single man or woman, starting from scratch in the insurance industry, could make it if he or she

had as little as $10,000 in personal savings or funding. No, I didn't forget a zero. I'm dead serious. You might have to rent space in an executive suite with a shared receptionist to answer the phones, and you might have to eat your lunches out of a paper sack for a while. But the beauty of the insurance business, as opposed to opening a franchise or traditional storefront, is that the start-up costs are not exorbitant. It only takes about two to three months before commission revenues start coming in from the insurance carriers. So, if you could survive for a couple of months on $10,000, you could literally open your own agency for less than the price of a typical used car.

While this is an insurance industry example, we all know people or have read stories about entrepreneurs who have gone from rags to riches. No matter if you are selling tacos, vehicles, repairing computers or mowing yards, the key to success is in how wisely you invest your money and how willing you are to beat the streets for business.

Now, I'm certainly not suggesting that you intentionally start out with a limited amount of capital. But I am saying that you should not be intimidated by limited resources. As Norman Vincent Peale once said, "Empty pockets never held anyone back. Only empty heads and empty hearts can do that."

Besides, receiving funding isn't nearly as difficult as most people think. Many people tend to believe that borrowing money is a tremendous obstacle. It isn't. In fact, depending on your credit history and rating, it isn't an obstacle at all. And even if your credit rating isn't sparkling, money is available. You just need to take the proper steps to locate it and secure it.

As I have previously mentioned, planning is absolutely critical in virtually every aspect of your business. This is especially true in terms of funding for your business. With that said, allow me to introduce Mike Weisenburger, who manages the business lending partnership with Nationwide Bank in an effort to assist agents with their agency expansion. The Ohio-based Weisenburger has also served prominent roles with credit unions; he has overseen the credit card/electronic banking products for traditional banks; and he has more than 35 years of experience in the financial services industry. Weisenburger has sat across the desk from countless entrepreneurs who have entered his office with big dreams and big financial requests. His financial expertise would be invaluable to any entrepreneur, especially one who is looking to start or expand an insurance agency. So, I posed the following question to Mike: "What's the No. 1 tip you could provide for a perspective business owner?" His sage answer: "Have a rich dad."

He was joking. Sort of. Weisenburger has personally seen his fair share of successes. He has approved the loans of substantial sums of money to both start-up agents and established ones, who have used the funding to generate sizeable profits and achieve their financial objectives. Unfortunately, he's also seen his fair share of failures—mostly due to a lack of preparation. According to Weisenburger, the first step you need to take after you have your dreams and goals written down is to make sure your personal life is in order. In other words, your family must be on board before you even begin thinking about setting sail.

"In my dealings, I've come to realize that those who have a stable personal life have a better chance of succeeding," Weisenburger said. "Too often, I've seen people coming in asking for funding because they are sick of the corporate world and want to go into business for themselves. But the first step is to have your personal plan and career in line, which means your family has to be on board. If you're single and just starting off, that's a different story. But if you are married and you have kids, they need to be on board before you come asking for funding. You have to realize it's going to be seven days a week, twenty-four hours a day for five years or more as you get your program up and running. You've got to have the support of your family, and—this is very important—understand what you need to support your existing living expenses. One of the things we see over and over with new or expanding business owners is that they don't realize how much money it takes to support their lifestyle today."

"We've seen men and women seeking funding who are leaving $150,000 per year jobs, who think they can step back to $50,000 per year income. Yet, they are not willing to give up the large house, the country club or the big car. Neither is their spouse. So, what you do personally to prepare to find your funding is probably as important as having a great business plan. You need your family's support. I don't know of very many people who come in here saying, "I'm going to do whatever it takes, even if it costs me my family." Most people come in here wanting to do something better for their family, but they do not account for the sacrifices it is going to take."

"You've got to know what all is involved, not just how to sell insurance," Weisenburger continued. "You've also got to know what it takes to run your business as the principal. We've seen executives come to us straight from the 40th floor of their nice corner office, who are now going to run their own agency. But they have forgotten that, as a business owner, they will now need to pay the electrical bill, shovel the snow off the sidewalk and call the repairman when the air conditioning doesn't work. They forgot how to coordinate the financial ins and outs of their company and have never done human resources. Now they have to be HR managers, operational managers, sales managers and the lead salesperson.

FAMILY

They have to be capable of wearing many hats. They need to have good financial accounting advice, a tax plan and a good attorney. But I think the very first step is making sure that their family knows what is involved. And their family must understand that it is not going to be easy, it's not going to happen overnight, and it's probably going to be financially, emotionally and physically draining for several years."

I wholeheartedly agree. In fact, I believe the first and most important sales job you must make prior to entering this industry is to your spouse and family. If you need help designing a family budget or would like to examine some methods of controlling household spending, review the website at **www.gameplanbook.com.** 👉

I can afford to drive a Mercedes Benz and live in the house of my dreams now. But it certainly wasn't always that way. When Lisa and I started in this industry—notice that it wasn't just me; it was a partnership right from the start—our meals often consisted of either Tuna or Hamburger Helper®. We dreamed of going out for prime rib, but when we actually went out to eat, it was often for a McRib®. It wasn't always easy, and it sure as hell wasn't always tasty. But we asked ourselves on a daily basis: "Are we willing to sacrifice for our business? And are we willing to sacrifice for however long it takes?" I sold Lisa on the promise of a brighter future and the benefits of delayed gratification long before I sold a policy.

So, why is this such an important first step? Because I am firmly convinced that you will find business funding. A five-figure or six-figure check will soon be in your hands. You can practically bank on that if you prepare properly. But how conservatively you handle that funding—and how you prepare yourself and your family to view that money—is what will likely determine your business success or failure. I've seen far too many people in this industry—and many others—who have chosen to use borrowed money extravagantly. They get a six-figure check that is supposed to sustain their business for the next couple of years, and they instantly become as flamboyant as Donald Trump's interior decorator.

Not too long ago, I received a call from a woman who had done some auditing work with our agency. When she was working with us, she seemed sharp; she appeared to have a nose for the business; and she certainly seemed to have a strong work ethic. It wasn't until she received a $300,000 loan from an insurance company that I realized she actually had a lump of Spam® for a brain.

Perhaps that sounds callous and cruel on my part. And admittedly, this woman's issue was not a lack of intelligence; it was a lack of preparation and planning. When she received that $300,000 loan, she simply didn't have the discipline to manage the money conservatively. She immediately went to an upscale department store to purchase all of her office furniture and fixtures, believing that she needed to impress her prospects with the appearance of her office. But that's like the owner of a new construction company purchasing his hammers from Neiman Marcus. You make your strongest impression on customers with the quality of your service, not the décor of your office. The point here is that this particular woman spent so much money on an attractive office that she didn't have enough left to go out and attract customers. Just six months into her business, she could see the handwriting on her elaborately decorated walls.

She called me and told me that things were not working out. Initially, I was surprised because I would have predicted that she would have made a strong insurance agent. And she probably would have if she had not treated that loan like lottery winnings. She asked me if I might be interested in buying her out and taking over her lease. I said I would love to talk to her and casually asked how much money she had invested in setting up the office. She had spent $125,000—more than a third of her total loan amount. I was astounded and no longer surprised that she was on her way out. Be prepared to handle your funding with extreme caution, care and conservatism. Don't be surprised by the fact that some lender is willing to take a chance on you, even if you have never been handed a lump sum of cash in the past. Remember that it's merely seed money. Plant it wisely, and you will grow an impressive crop. Spread it foolishly, and you will inevitably be in a mess of crap.

Okay, I'll come down from this particular soap box for now and move onto the next step of your planning. It's imperative that you sit down with a pencil, a calculator and a telephone to begin estimating exactly how much you need. As Weisenburger said, you will need an accountant and an attorney. Talk to your associates; talk to your circle of friends; and talk to your neighbors about who they know in these industries. Then pick up the phone and inquire about their rates and services.

You may also need an office location or storefront. Here again, I encourage you to think conservatively, especially if you are in start-up mode. You don't need a penthouse suite or a prime piece of real estate to be successful. You've probably heard that in the restaurant business the three keys to success are: location, location, location. I don't necessarily agree. How many hole-in-the-wall restaurants are thriving? How many times have you gone out of the way—far off the beaten path—to find the restaurant you've heard about from your friends and associates? It happens all the time. And location is even less important in the insurance industry. You are not going to spend a whole lot of time inside that office anyway. If you want to be successful, you are going to be driving customers to your business location, not vice-versa.

Far too many start-up businesses fail because the owners expect customers to find them on their own. It's not going to happen that way. Your success is going to be determined by what you do outside your business walls, so don't waste any more than you need on them. Think small; think conservatively; and think about all the other expenses associated with a location. In addition to your lease, you will need to pay for utilities, office phone lines, Internet connections, website design costs, software fees, furniture, fixtures, and cell phone expenses, etc. Here again, the only way to find out about these costs is to pick up the phone and start calling. Check out the newspaper ads for prospective locations; talk to commercial realtors; ask your friends and associates for leads. Then call to find out about the up-front costs, as well as the hidden ones. Is a security system in place? How about extermination fees? Landscaping dues? Parking fees? The only way to determine how much money you need is to be as thorough as possible.

Depending on your type of business, you may also need to find someone to answer the phones, which is why an executive suite or an answering service might be good options for starting off. There's really no point in hiring an office assistant until you are actually driving business into your office. But it is wise to plan in advance for that day. Again, think conservatively. You don't need to pay someone $40,000 a year to answer your phones and handle your appointment book. To this day, I still have entry level employees working for me for less than $20,000 per year. If they prove themselves, you can award a raise at a later date.

Then there's the marketing budget to consider. You must have a number and details for your financier to evaluate. How are you going to get the word out about your business? How much is an ad in your local Yellow Pages? How about newspaper ads? Direct mail? Flyers? We'll cover strategies and techniques in a later chapter, but the bottom line here is that you must have a number.

You also need to plan to put yourself on the payroll. Far too many people use their business capital to pay expenses and then keep the rest for themselves. That's a recipe for disaster. Put yourself on a salary that meets your family's needs, and then give yourself a raise or bonus only when you achieve your goals.

Once you have all of these business and personal expenses on paper, you are ready to determine how much money you need to seek in a loan. But before you do, consider these wise words from Weisenburger: "Put a financial plan together and then double it," he said. "Do not be conservative here. Every time you turn around, somebody else wants another check. If you've never run a business, you better research it. Talk to the successful people you know, and don't forget to talk to those who have failed. You can learn as much from those who have failed as you can from those who have flourished. In many cases, those who failed simply did not realize how much it costs to get started. You must be completely prepared before you ever go seeking a loan."

At this point, you may be discouraged. That little voice may be trying to convince you that there is too much to consider, too many variables, too many expenses, etc. Take a deep breath and repeat after me: "I've got what it takes."

Most of the population gets bogged down in the details. That's why most of the population has little—if any—financial security. Keep the big picture in mind, and keep your dreams in front of you. This can be a tedious process and a difficult one. But it is not impossible. In fact, it is quite possible if you will just follow through with the steps. In other words, just do it.

I encourage you to stop reading right here and start putting pen to paper. It may take you a couple of days to put your personal and business budget together. That's fine. I'll be here when you get back. If you need assistance in this endeavor, please refer to our website at **www.gameplanbook.com.**

It will provide valuable resources for you. Sit down with your spouse; sit down with your kids; consider every possible source of income that you now have to mitigate your risks; and cover all the potential costs that you may incur. Put it all down on paper, and then we'll begin covering where to go and what to do to receive your funding.

WHERE TO FIND YOUR MONEY

Okay, I'm going to assume that you at least have a rough budget outline. You can fine tune it as we go along, but it's essential that you have something on paper before moving forward. Remember, you are much more likely to find someone to loan you money or invest in your business if you have a detailed business and financial plan supporting your requests.

Now, the next question is: Where do you go to find that funding? The most traditional route is through a banker, and that's certainly a good option. But the key here is to be thoroughly prepared before you ever go sit down with the banker. And the first step in being prepared is to have your business plan in place. Don't be afraid to borrow money, and don't be hesitant to borrow ideas in pursuit of financing.

BUDGET When you sit down with that banker, your best bet, especially if you are starting off, is to start with your local community bank. Those are the folks who live in your community and are typically going to be more committed to the community where you are going to establish your business. They will be committed to your success, and they will be more readily available to you when you need them. Of course, if you already have an existing relationship with a banker or loan officer, start with him or her. And right from the start, remember this: Getting turned down for financing is not the end of your dreams. In most cases, it can be very beneficial in terms of sharpening your focus, your business plan, etc.

Many sales trainers have told me that you need to be told "no" at least six times before you quit asking. I would suggest that you ask the lender in a different way each time and provide different information. But you've got to keep asking. I've been turned down on ideas many, many times, but I'll go back to the plan, manipulate it, revise it and go back to the lender to ask them in a different way. Hear what the lender says; ask questions about why you are being turned down; be composed at all times and do not—I repeat, DO NOT—burn any bridges when seeking financing. I've already mentioned that my temper can be difficult to manage at times, and I have been on the verge of lashing out at lenders who rejected my proposals. But I've bitten my tongue and benefited in the long run.

Burning bridges is the stupidest thing you can do. I don't care if that lender tells you that your business plan is the worst he or she has ever seen. Stay calm and ask him or her, "What can make it better?" What you are doing here is not only fine-tuning your plan; you're also building a relationship with that lender. The next time you sit in that office, you will have a plan that is more suited to pique the interest of that particular lender. You will have also proven to him or her that you have the persistence, the patience and the perseverance to handle the rejections and objections that will ultimately come your way in business. It's a long-term test, so be prepared to meet with that particular lender five or six times before you scrap that plan and go in another lending direction.

Another thing to remember before you sit down with a banker is that not all money is the same. There are two types of funding: equity and debt. When you are seeking money, your debt-to-equity ratio will play a large role in whether you receive start-up financing

or not. The more money (equity) you have
personally invested in your business, the easier
it will be to find attractive debt financing from
a bank, savings and loan, commercial finance
company, an insurance provider, manufacture or
even the U.S. Small Business Administration.

I already know what you're thinking: If I had
enough money to invest in my business, I
wouldn't need a banker or any other kind of
debt financing!

Stay calm. There are many ways to skin
a cat and many ways to make your equity
look fat. According to the SBA, most small
or growth-stage businesses use limited equity
financing, and additional equity often comes
from non-professional investors such as friends,
relatives, employees, customers or industry colleagues. I, for one,
have been down that road.

I've borrowed money from my sister, father-in-law and
friends. I encourage you to look around your circle of friends,
family, associates, etc. to look for potential investors. But do
it professionally. Approach it as a mutually beneficial business
transaction, not as a favor from your family member, workout partner
or fellow church parishioner.

I took my sister a promissory note when I was starting out and told
her that I wanted to borrow $25,000. I told her that I would pay it
back over five years and presented her with the terms. I had all the
paperwork in place before I went to her. If I would have defaulted
on that, she could have written it off showing documentation of bad
debt. If you've burned your family in the past, they probably won't
loan you money, but if your intentions are to use the money to grow
the business they'll probably help you. I didn't go beg her for it,
either. I went to her and talked about what we wanted to do. I also
pointed out that I would pay her a higher interest rate on the loan than
she could make from a bank CD. It was a smart financial investment

for her, and it added immediate equity to my business. So, if one banker is telling you that you have too high of a proportion of debt-to-equity, start looking around to see where you might be able to increase your ownership capital.

The reason many people fail when they seek an individual investor is because they find a successful associate and say something like, "I want you to invest in my company." I've had friends approach me like this. But in reality, I don't have any interest in investing in their company. On the other hand, I would be far more interested in your proposal if you came to me and said, "I would like to borrow $50,000, and I'll pay you a 7 percent interest rate. I'll pay you the money back in 36 months." Now, I'm interested. You are going to pay more than the bank because there is more at risk. But you are more likely to receive the loan because we have a pre-existing relationship, and I will not require the security like the bank will.

Many insurance companies, manufacturers, franchisors or distributors have capital available for starting or expanding your business. That funding, however, may be a little harder to find if you are starting an agency or new business. These types of investors are not typically going to step up and loan you money when you've never sold their products, goods or services. But if you are an established representative looking to expand, this is an outstanding source of debt funding. I would guess that I've borrowed more than $2 million in funding from insurance companies to grow our business. I'll simply write a business plan and start floating it around until I find someone who is willing to help me pursue my objectives with the necessary funding. If you put the insurance company's logo and branding on the plan and you have a solid track record, then they are often receptive to your plan. You just have to ask for it. And—I am going to beat a dead horse here—  you just have to be composed about any rejections that may arise.

Even if you are an experienced agent, you will be rejected.

For example, when I wrote the plan in 2002 for Nationwide Insurance to grow my business. We were looking to open several stores for them, and I was seeking the funding from them to do this. I provided them with the business plan, and I had a Nationwide person in my office every time I could. I started showing them that business plan, and I finally got them to agree to loan me the money. It was a performance-based loan, where if I reached a certain point and generated enough new policies, the loan would be forgiven. But if I didn't reach the goals, I would have to pay the money back. We did great with the first block of money, and the business was growing, so I went back and asked for more money. They agreed, and they also waved about half of the money that I had borrowed from them. Then I borrowed more than $1 million to do the next phase. I refinanced the $300,000 that I owed them from the first deal and tacked on another $780,000. They divided the money into segments and wanted a certain performance. Well, we had some trouble getting the stores open, and they weren't performing as well as we had hoped. There were also some market changes, and it became clear that we weren't going to be able to reach our targeted numbers. To make a long story shorter, I didn't receive the next segment of money. I was very disappointed and extremely frustrated. I believed that Nationwide had instituted some changes that played a major role in us not reaching our numbers. I wanted to lash out. Instead, I kept working different angles. I eventually met with a senior executive of the company, and I calmly asked for her to reconsider the loan. A few days later, the loan was approved. The point here is that I could have accepted "no." I also could have burned some bridges. Instead, I practiced what I am now preaching to you. I kept approaching people, providing them with reasons why they should provide me this money. I was told "no" five or six times before I was told "yes."

Where there is a will, there is a way. And if a time arises when there seems like no way, check out American Express. From personal experience, I have found that American Express will loan you more money with less restrictions than any other organization I have ever come across. It may take you a while before your business is large enough for a bank to be truly interested in you. But if you have any kind of decent credit history, call on American Express. In many cases, you could probably receive a $30,000 unsecured line of credit in a couple of days. You don't need a business plan to go through American Express: your good name will secure that line of credit. You can do the same with VISA, MasterCard, or any other line of credit account. I started with American Express, and I still use it for practically every expense because of the benefits it provides me. I recently planned a trip to San Francisco, and I called the Four Seasons, which quoted me a room rate of $415 per night. I then called American Express and asked what kind of deals they had at the Four Seasons in San Francisco. They could get me the same room for $385 with a free breakfast, free lunch, an upgraded room if available at check-in, and late check-out at 4 p.m. I paid $30 less for the room and they set it up. Plus, I paid for my airline tickets with points from American Express.

There's nothing wrong with having some business debt. In fact, borrowing money—and then having the discipline to pay it back—can be a tremendous long-term benefit for your future growth. The funding may be difficult to find at first, but it is available. If you pay it back promptly and establish a strong financial track record, lenders will begin seeking you.

Do your financial homework, get your family on board, cover all possible obstacles and objections, fine-tune your business plan and your personal budget, build relationships with lending organizations and then DO NOT be afraid to ask for financing. In other words: Just Do It.

GAME DAY PREP

1. Many people fail to take the necessary action steps to build a business because:
   A. They lack official Nike gear.
   B. They are too busy making New Year's resolutions.
   C. Their sense of urgency is really gas.
   D. They are afraid to even seek business funding because they assume no one will loan them any money.

   Answer here _____

2. When seeking business funding, you should start off by going to:
   A. The largest, most impersonal, commercial bank you can find.
   B. A local community bank or non-professional investors such as friends, relatives, employees, customers or industry colleagues.
   C. A company you do business with or a manufacturer whose product you represent.
   D. Either B or C, but certainly not A.

   Answer here _____

3. When a potential lender or investor turns you down, you should:
   A. Give them the finger and put sugar in their gas tank.
   B. Throw all your plans and dreams out the window because you obviously suck.
   C. Take the positives and negatives from the meeting, revise and fine-tune your plan, continue to build relationships with lenders, re-present your plan and never give up.

D. Go to the liquor store, purchase a fifth of something and howl at the moon.

Answer here_____

More detailed information about the topics covered in this chapter is available at www.gameplanbook.com.

The website is continually updated to provide the latest information, forms, instructions and tips to help you build or grow your business.

Extra Points - Notes

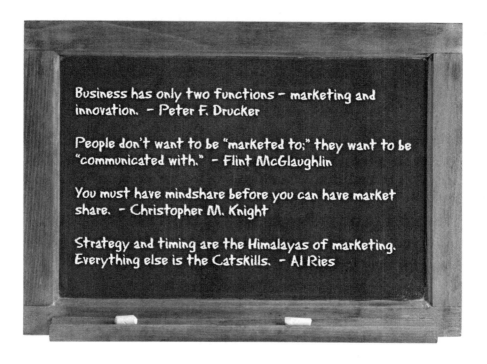

Business has only two functions – marketing and innovation. – Peter F. Drucker

People don't want to be "marketed to," they want to be "communicated with." – Flint McGlaughlin

You must have mindshare before you can have market share. – Christopher M. Knight

Strategy and timing are the Himalayas of marketing. Everything else is the Catskills. – Al Ries

CHAPTER 3

ACTIVATE YOUR MARKETING

Just for fun, I recently went to Yahoo's home page and typed into its search engine the following question: "What is marketing?" It gave me a few web pages to review. Five hundred and forty-three million, to be exact. I did the same with Google, and typed in, "How to market your business." The feedback: 273 million websites. Finally, I went to MSN and typed the words: "Business marketing tips." My search returned a paltry 16 million results.

So, naturally, I proceeded to spend the next 37 years of my life reviewing all 832 million websites that my searches had returned.

Yeah, right. If I wanted to waste my life away, I'd take the more direct route and contemplate who built the great pyramids (Amway and Mary Kay, not the ones in Egypt).

Marketing seems like such a simple word, but it is actually one of the most misunderstood and confused concepts in the business world today. Millions of people have an opinion on it. Hundreds of thousands of people consider themselves to be experts on the subject. Thousands of colleges across the country offer degree programs in it. And yet, if I walked onto the downtown streets of Houston—or any other large city in the United States, for that matter—it would probably be difficult to find many business people who had a true handle on it. And I am betting that I would be hard-pressed to find even a handful of marketing department people who would give me the same definition of what good marketing really encompasses.

Why? Because the word "marketing" invokes so many different images. Some people see billboards; others see TV commercials; some see direct mail pieces; and others see images in the newspaper. Some people think about catchphrases; others hear jingles. Many people hear the word "marketing," and they envision glitzy campaigns, big corporate budgets and board rooms filled with sharp-dressed Donald Trump wannabes and quick-witted, creative women who are as sharp as their stilettos. Marketing, in the minds of many people, is a high-stakes, big-dollar endeavor.

FOOD = SALES

To me, however, the word marketing—at least how it applies to my own insurance business—brings to mind images of submarine sandwiches. Or a couple of boxes of donuts. Or candy bars. No, I'm not referring to Rosie O'Donnell's daily dietary intake here. These simple food items are some of my most valuable marketing tools. They can be highly effective for you, as well—regardless of whether you are starting out or expanding an established organization.

Marketing is absolutely essential to your business success and growth, but it doesn't need to be expensive. Let me repeat that again: You do not need to spend mega bucks to receive a big bang on your marketing efforts. In fact, I am firmly convinced that you can accomplish about as much with a box of donuts as you can with a billboard on the busiest interstate in your community.

Before I go any further with my marketing "food for thought," let me make one thing perfectly clear: Marketing and advertising are not the same things. That's one of the biggest misconceptions of marketing. According to Jon Spoelstra, author of *Ice to the Eskimos* and *Marketing Outrageously*, advertising is an important component of marketing. But advertising and marketing are not one in the same. In other words, you can market successfully without advertising. Advertising without marketing, however, is just plain stupid.

I've never actually seen any businessmen dumping truckloads of money onto the interstate during rush-hour traffic. Nor have I seen any businesswomen driving through neighborhoods while emptying trash bags filled with cash onto front lawns. But, in essence, this is exactly what many well-meaning entrepreneurs do when they pour their precious start-up capital or hard-earned business profits unnecessarily into advertising. If you think a billboard with a picture of yourself is going to drive customers to your business, you're wrong. If you believe that expensive newspaper or magazine ads will make you an overnight success, you're sadly mistaken. And if you are tempted to pay big bucks to put your face on grocery store shopping carts, you will likely only end up with egg on your face. Literally and figuratively.

Don't get me wrong. Advertising can boost your marketing and sales efforts. And there is most definitely a time and a place for it, as I will discuss later in this chapter. It is not, however, the sole answer in getting your phone to ring or bringing new customers into your business. Especially from a start-up perspective, it is often nothing more than a waste of time and money. Let me assure you that as soon as you open your doors, advertising salespeople will call you. They will offer you the opportunity to hear your name on the radio and to see your face on TV. They will provide you with fabulous packages and incentives. They will promise you that your name will be heard by numerous listeners and your company logo will be in front of countless targeted readers. They will tell you that your sign or billboard will be seen by this many commuters or that many drivers stuck in morning traffic. But even if what they say is absolutely true, it probably won't cause your phone to ring.

Think about billboards, for example. When is the last time a billboard actually caused you to take action? I'm not talking about taking notice; I'm talking about taking action. Chances are very good that the last time a billboard caused you to do something was when you were driving from one city to another, and you felt severe hunger pangs. If you see a McDonald's billboard while on a four-hour road trip, you may wind up at McDonald's because of that particular sign. But let's say you see that same sign in your own hometown. Does it cause you to go to McDonald's? Probably not. And how about that beer billboard? So many of the leading beer companies have decided that the best way to appeal to the beer-gutted men out there is to use flat-bellied, bikini-wearing women in their ads. Some of the beer billboards feature models who are so darned centerfold-sexy that they ought to include staples. As a result, you may notice the billboard, but does it actually cause you to buy that particular brand? Probably not.

I love the Bud Light® and Miller Lite® advertisements, but they do not cause me to change my beer of preference, Coors Light®. It's strictly awareness advertising, and big companies like Budweiser, Coca-Cola, McDonald's, Dodge, etc. spend billions of advertising dollars each year making sure that consumers like you and me are aware of their products. The insurance companies are no different. Allstate spends millions to make sure that consumers know that they are "In Good Hands." Nationwide advertises nationally to spread the message that it is *"On Your Side®."* And unless you have been living under a rock, you are undoubtedly quite familiar with the AFLAC duck and the GEICO gecko. That little lizard has become a national icon. But does the world's most recognizable reptile really cause you to switch your current auto coverage to GEICO? Not if you're satisfied with your current provider.

According to the 2006 National Auto Insurance Study conducted by J.D. Power and Associates, Amica ranked highest in overall customer satisfaction among 14,066 auto insurance policyholders for the seventh consecutive year.

On its own corporate website, Amica states in a press release: "Perhaps you've never heard of Amica. If Northwest Mutual is the quiet company, Amica seems almost mute." The release ends with: "Amica not only has policyholders—(it has) organic word-of-mouth marketers. When you have superb service, you don't need to throw millions out the window making 30 seconds of noise (advertisements) during the Super Bowl."

I wholeheartedly agree from a corporate standpoint. And from an individual businessowner's standpoint, word-of-mouth is the way to go. You don't necessarily need to be on the radio; you don't even need people to remember your name. Your goal should be to become known in your circle of influence as "the insurance guy," "the dry cleaning guy," "the landscaping guy," etc. And to do that, I want you to think differently than most agents or businessowners do. You have undoubtedly heard the term "Think outside the box." But from a marketing standpoint, I encourage you to "think inside the donut box." And, for now, I am going to assume that you are A) starting out as a small business owner; B) trying to invest wisely as you grow your business; or C) not an heiress to the Hilton family's financial empire. If you have an endless amount of money to burn on image/awareness advertising, skip on to the next chapter. You won't need any of these tips to get noticed.

FORGET YOUR FAMILY AND THE FRONT DOOR

Still reading? Okay, then I am led to believe that managing your marketing budget and keeping expenses to a minimum are important issues to you. Two of the biggest mistakes that most business owners make when they open their doors are

1) assuming that putting a sign up in a strip center will cause clients to come in and 2) that their friends and family members should be their first prospects. Wrong. On both accounts.

Once you open your doors for business, plan to hit the streets to find clients or customers. Once in a blue moon, a customer will wander through your doors and announce that

MARKETING = ACTION

he/she needs your products or services. But as a general rule of thumb, prospects will not find you; you must find them. DO NOT assume that even the fabulous, flamboyant sign over your business door will draw customers to you. You need to find them. Of course, as soon as I tell aspiring business owners that, they immediately tend to view their friends and family members as their top initial prospects. I urge you not to go down this road. Let your family members—and friends, for that matter—eventually come to you. This will alleviate plenty of heartache and headaches down the road. When you solicit business from your family members, you are only asking for trouble. They can tend to be your most tedious and demanding clients, especially if they perceive that they are doing you a favor by doing business with you. So, my advice to you is not to try to sell to them. Simply allow them to come to you as your business grows. It will eventually happen.

So, where do you start to find your prospects? And then how do you market to them? You merely need to go talk to people. Don't sit in your office, your showroom, your restaurant, etc. The art of selling is contacting people, and the art of marketing is having contacts. As part of a marketing plan, I encourage my salespeople to join a networking group. I also encourage them to be a regular attendee at a Chamber of Commerce breakfast, which is typically a weekly affair. And if you happen to be at a party, please, please, please do not spend the entire time talking to the people you already know. Meet new people. Grab new business cards. It's not difficult. Walk up to a person, extend you hand, introduce yourself and ask him/her what he/she does for a living. That's all there is to it. In these settings, you will inevitably meet mortgage bankers, realtors, automobile salesmen and many people of influence. When you get to know these folks, you have contacts.

Let's say, for example, that you meet an automobile salesman at a party on Saturday night. Some small-minded insurance agents might think: "Hey, here's an opportunity to sell a policy to this particular man or woman." But the big-picture thinker says to himself: "This is a contact who could lead me to hundreds of policies." You need to think big and to begin marketing with donut money instead of big dough.

After you have engaged the car salesman and taken a business card, call him on Monday and tell him you enjoyed meeting him the other night. After a little small talk, ask him who he typically sends his customers to for auto insurance. When he tells you who he sends customers to, ask him why and let him know that you may be able to help him grow his business. Next, ask him if he thinks that customers generally arrive at the dealership knowing what they can afford to pay for the car? The answer, of course, is "yes." This leads you into an easy dialogue that I am going to provide for you here.

YOU: Of course, they do. And the smart customer, the one who is really serious about buying a vehicle, probably also has an understanding of what he is going to need to pay for auto insurance each month, right?

JOE SALESMAN: Right.

YOU: Many serious buyers will call an insurance provider before they even show up at the dealership, especially if they are moving to a sports car or upgrading from their current vehicle, to see exactly how much higher the insurance premiums might be, right?

JOE SALESMAN: Yes. What's your point?

YOU: My point is that if I can beat the auto insurance rate that they have been quoted, then you have a better chance of actually putting them in that car.

63

JOE SALESMAN: Okay, you've got me interested now. Continue.

YOU: Well, let's say that the customer has budgeted $500 a month for a new car and the insurance ($400 for the car and $100 for the insurance). But you do the numbers and come back from the sales tower with a car payment of $480 a month, not including insurance. So, the client says he can't do that, because in his mind he is assuming his total cost is going to be $580 ($480 for the car payment and $100 for insurance), which puts him $80 over budget. At this point, you call our office and get a rate from me to see if I can save him some money on insurance. If I can save him $30 each month on insurance and you can come down to $430 a month, he's probably going to go for that deal. So, he's in a new car, you've

made a sale that grossed $30 more a month than he was initially willing to spend, and I've got a policy that I am committed to servicing. The car is probably going to be financed for five years, which means $30 x 60 months over what he was initially willing to spend. So, you've just grossed up that car by $1,800. Everybody's happy.

JOE SALESMAN: Can you really do that?

YOU: Of course I can. What time do you open Thursday morning?

JOE SALESMAN: 10 a.m.

YOU: Get two or three of your salesmen buddies together at 9 a.m., and I will meet you at the dealership then. I'll bring breakfast, and we'll discuss how we can help each other close more deals.

JOE SALESMAN: Great. I'll have the coffee ready. Come in the service door; the front doors aren't open until 10.

Okay, now here's your opportunity to make an impression. You have bypassed the front door where secretaries are generally trained to turn you away and have been offered entrance into the service or back door. Now, here's the next key to building your business without busting your bank account. Do not try to impress them by bringing in a four-course breakfast. Bring a box of donuts or sausage kolaches. The impression you will leave with them will have everything to do with how you can help them make more sales, not by how much you spend on breakfast. Feed them with information, and don't go overboard with spending money on food. And remember this: If you want to sell 20 auto insurance units a week, all you need are a handful of salesmen sending potential clients to you. Your entire sales pitch to them is that you can help them close deals. It's the same situation with realtors and mortgage bankers. I included an insurance example here to get you to think of ways to utilize centers of influence to drive customers to your business. It's about them (the centers of influence), not you.

Okay, let's look at another potential scenario. Let's say you meet a small business owner at a Chamber of Commerce function and strike a connection. You exchange business cards and call him in a couple of days. Ask him if you can sponsor a lunch for his employees sometime in the next week. Most small business owners will jump at this opportunity because it keeps his employees in the office (less down time) and it is often perceived by his staff as an unexpected benefit. Sponsoring a lunch happens frequently in all sorts of businesses, but the typical insurance agent—or the restaurant owner, the mortgage broker, the body shop owner, the carwash spokesperson, etc.—fails to truly market to the small business owner's staff. It's nothing more than a gigantic waste of time and money to sponsor a lunch and then to leave business cards, menus or coupons in the break room next to the sandwiches and sodas that you just purchased. This is half-active marketing at its absolute worst. You might—and let me emphasize the word "might"—receive a phone call or a letter from a secretary, thanking you for providing the staff lunch. But the chances of you selling anything are slim…if not none.

What you actually want is the opportunity to market actively to the business owner's staff. And to do that, you need to take full opportunity of the business owner opening his back door to you to carry the food into the break room. You have a captive audience, so capture it. Have a plan of attack to make yourself memorable.

Let's start off with the menu. Instead of buying 12 or 13 individual sandwiches, purchase three or four longer subs and have them cut into finger-food portions. If I provide you with an entire sandwich, you will likely eat it all. But if I give you a four-inch slice of a sandwich, you will eat that without complaining because, after all, it's free. Bring the sodas, chips and pies, as well. Just slice the pies into slivers and bring a couple of big bags of chips instead of 12 individual bags. Remember, you want them to feast on your information and snack on the food. Don't go overboard. It's just not necessary. Now, do your homework and plan to go to work. Have a game plan that includes your personal commercial. Don't waste time telling them about yourself. They don't care. What they will care about is how you can help them, how you can protect their investments, how you can solve their problems and how you can meet their needs better than the next guy or the last guy. Focus on them, not you.

What you have just done in that situation is a prime example of active marketing. If I had walked into that office and said, "Here's lunch and remember, *Nationwide is On Your Side*®," that would have been passive marketing. But by taking an active role in the lunch I just dramatically increased the potential of selling some policies. And even if I didn't sell a single policy at that moment or in the weeks to come, I have become known to those people as, "The Insurance Guy." By collecting their business cards, I also have a chance to send short, handwritten notes to each of them, reminding them of who I am and what services I provide. By spending $30 to

$40 on that lunch, I would have potentially made much more of an impact on those people than I could if I spent $5,000 on a billboard right outside their office. You can apply this example to practically any business.

Especially if you are starting off, I would not spend a single penny on passive or "awareness" marketing. Nothing. Depending on how much you can spend, I would try to budget at least $500 a month toward active marketing, and I would spend it all—at least in the early development stages—on food. Not just any food, but cheap food. Do not fall into the trap of justifying an expensive dinner at a fancy restaurant to impress a single prospective customer. That's typically a waste when you are in the early stages of growing your business. You can often do much, much more with carrot sticks and cola than caviar. Always keep your eyes open for other inexpensive and creative ways to actively market. I recently stole an idea from an auto body shop in Houston involving candy bars. The body shop was passing out candy bars with specialized wrappers featuring its corporate logo. Good idea, I thought. Then I took it a step further. For Valentine's Day, we had candy wrappers especially designed for the mortgage bankers and realtors we work with regularly. They were Hershey bars, but the wrapper featured our corporate logo on it and on the back, where the nutritional facts are normally listed, we included flood facts. We were promoting flood insurance, and our message included things such as: Sixty-five percent of the people who incurred flood damage from Tropical Storm Allison were outside the special flood area. It was a relatively inexpensive project, but it gave our agents a way to interact with current and prospective circles of influence. We didn't just drop them at the receptionist's stand; we walked into these businesses and handed them out individually. When people eat chocolate, they tend to be in a better mood, so if you're the one giving them the chocolate, they are in a better mood because of you.

Before we actually address any actual advertising techniques (yes I do believe in some traditional advertising at the right time and place), I want to provide another example for you to consider. At some point in time you will be contacted by a local charitable organization to help sponsor something. I do my best to give back to the community, and I highly advise you to do the same. But keep in mind that there are ways to support your community and actively promote your business at the same time. For example, the tried-and-true charitable golf tournament.

You will be approached to sponsor a golf tournament. Mark my words on that. The organizers of the tournament are usually in search of a check from you to be a title sponsor, a hole sponsor, etc. Many people will simply write a check for $250, $500, $1,000 or so forth out of the goodness of their hearts. For their money, they will likely receive the opportunity to play golf and will see their corporate logo somewhere on the course. A small sign will likely be placed near the tee area of each hole reading, "This hole sponsored by Greg the Dry Cleaner Guy." That's passive marketing; that's a tax write-off; that's a nice gesture on Greg's behalf; but that's not going to produce any sales for Greg. After all, can you remember any of the sponsors of the last tournament where you played? How about the last charity gala you attended? Probably not.

If I were counseling Greg, I would urge him to be a part of the charitable tournament, but I'd also encourage him to approach it from an active marketing position. If he had enough money to write a check, so be it. But even if he could write a check, I would tell him not to play golf, but rather, to work the hole. And if he didn't have the money to write a $1,000 check? That's fine, too. You can still have an extremely high-profile presence at the tournament while helping the charity. When the tournament organizer calls you,

68

tell him or her that you would like to be a part of it. Let's say that Tara Tournament Organizer is the one who calls. Here would be my conversation with her:

TARA TOURNAMENT ORGANIZER: Mr. Dry Cleaner Guy, we are hosting a golf tournament at the nearby country club on April 6 with all the proceeds going to cancer research in our community. The hole sponsor cost is $1,000. Can we count on your support?

YOU: Absolutely. That is such a great cause that I would love to be part of the tournament. But, quite frankly, I cannot at this time make that kind of financial commitment. But I can certainly help you out in other ways.

TARA TOURNAMENT ORGANIZER: What other ways?

YOU: Well, first of all, I'll buy an insurance policy for the hole-in-one contest. I'm not going to pay you any money directly, but we'll sponsor a hole and put $20,000 cash on that hole. If someone makes a hole in one, the insurance policy will cover the payout. Then I'm going to show up at the hole with my digital camera. I'll take pictures of all the foursomes coming through, and will mail them the glossy pictures later that night (the printed photos will make a stronger impression than a photo that is e-mailed, and will often end up framed on a bookshelf in a business owner's office). I'll have a sign-up sheet where they can give me their contact information or they can simply hand me a business card. In addition to the $20,000 hole-in-one prize, I'll run a side game on the hole, as well.

TARA TOURNAMENT ORGANIZER: What kind of side game?

YOU: I will tell each golfer that we're trying to raise some additional money for further cancer research or a particular cancer patient. You decide. It will be $10 per person, and the golfer closest to the pin on that hole in that foursome puts his name in a hat. After the tourney is over, we're going to pull a name out of the hat and whoever gets his or her name drawn receives a free round for four at another golf course.

TARA TOURNAMENT ORGANIZER: We already have a closest-to-the-pin contest.

YOU: This wouldn't interfere with that. It would be an additional game. How many golfers are you expecting for the tournament?

TARA TOURNAMENT ORGANIZER: We have a morning round and an afternoon round with 72 golfers in each. So, 144 golfers total.

YOU: Great. Well, if everyone participated in this little side game, it would bring you an additional $1,440. And if 75 percent of them participated, it would still result in an additional $1,080. From that total, I will pay for the additional round for four players at another golf course, which I can probably get for around $250. So, you will net something in the neighborhood between $830 and $1,190. That alone would cover my hole sponsorship. Plus, I'd provide the policy for the hole-in-one contest. I'd also provide the golfers with photos. Does that sound like a win-win situation?

TARA TOURNAMENT ORGANIZER: Indeed, it does. Thank you very much.

YOU: You are quite welcome. All I ask for is a little time on the microphone after the tournament—during the awards presentation—to draw the winning name out of the hat.

TARA TOURNAMENT ORGANIZER: No problem. See you on April 6. It's a shotgun start at 8 a.m. You can have hole No. 8, a par-3.

Now, you have the opportunity to truly do some active marketing. You will have a chance to meet all 144 golfers during the round. If you can afford to do it, you can have golf bag tags, cigars or trinkets made with your contact information on it. But that is not a necessity. You will have contact information for 144 potential clients or customers. You will be able to send them a letter thanking them for participating in the contest along with the glossy picture. You might even include a tagline at the bottom of your letter that says something like: The summer season is approaching. Have you cleaned and packed your winter clothing for summer storage? Make sure by calling Greg the Dry Cleaner Guy.

You also will have the opportunity to stand before the group at the awards ceremony and be introduced as, "the Dry Cleaner Guy." Now, who are the golfers more likely to remember? You? Or the other dry cleaner who sponsored hole No. 15 by simply writing a check for $1,000? He had his company logo on a sign; you had face time with 144 golfers and have their contact information for future reference.

The key to marketing is that you have to own what you do. In this particular scenario, you weren't the main sponsor of the tournament, but everyone knew who you were. Your total cost was minimal. If you're going to do something, you've got to do it right. You may not always have enough money to be the biggest sponsor at an event, but with a little creativity and entrepreneurship, you can make the biggest impact. After all, marketing gurus have for many years preached that if you can get your message in front of someone three times they are far more likely to remember who you are. (You have done that at the particular hole, at the closing ceremony and by sending a letter). And the big picture here is that you did more to help the tournament fund cancer research than anyone else who simply wrote out a $1,000 check. It's win-win all the way.

GENERATING LOW COST OR FREE PUBLICITY

In the book *Marketing Outrageously*, author Jon Spoelstra details his involvement with a minor-league baseball team called the Las Vegas Stars. Serving as a new marketing consultant to the Triple-A franchise (in 2001), Spoelstra began his job by meeting with the employees of the team that had been in existence for eighteen years. And he started his research by asking: What do you think of the nickname, "Stars?"

"I've always hated it," one of the employees of sixteen years told Spoelstra. "But that was the name of the team when I joined up."

"We're not really the Stars," another employee told him. "The stars of Las Vegas are the entertainment headliners at the casinos. We're a Triple-A baseball team. Very few of our players will even make it to the bigs."

The Stars, quite frankly, were a boring franchise before Mandalay Sports Entertainment purchased the team and hired Spoelstra as a consultant. As Spoelstra wrote, "If you made a list of the five most boring things to do in this world, you'd put going to a Stars game somewhere on the list."

A few weeks after being hired, Spoelstra gathered a few employees from the fledgling franchise for a spontaneous meeting. Here's the rest of the very intriguing story: "I said, Suppose, just suppose, we had to change the name of the team. What would we call it? I stood by the blackboard, ready to write down names—and was surprised by the flurry of names tossed at me faster than I could write. A lot of names featured some facet of gambling…we bogged down in these, so I suggested we steer away from gambling. After a few moments of silence, we picked up steam again. One name seemed to jump out at us: the "51s"—as in Area 51, the super-secret air force base about 100 miles north of Las Vegas, the very existence of which the government denies. Area 51 is where the air force developed its stealth bomber and where—rumor has it—the United States is trying to reverse engineer a captured alien space ship."

Spoelstra then hired a graphic artist to design a team logo, featuring an alien with the 51s name. Then the media got wind of it. They hated it.

"Now I was sure we were on the right track," Spoelstra wrote. "Within two months, we officially changed the name. At that time of year, December, the team had never before been mentioned in the media. The 51s, however, were featured in *Sports Illustrated, Time, USA Today, the New York Times* and, at last count, over 100 other newspapers in the United States. The 51s were even featured in the *Yomiuri Daily* in Tokyo. The local newspaper, the *Las Vegas Review-Journal*, invited its readers to vote on its website whether they liked the name or not. The biggest response they had ever received before was 12,000 votes on the Binion murder trial, which was as big in Las Vegas as O.J. Simpson was in the nation at large. The 51s received over 15,000 votes—and to our surprise, over 77 percent liked the name! People were starting to think that maybe this Triple A baseball team wouldn't be boring."

The point: Sometimes the best advertising doesn't cost a dime. Imagine what that franchise would have had to pay for an advertisement in *Sports Illustrated, Time, USA Today*, etc. But because of the name change—a little creativity—the team received nationwide media attention without spending any money.

Now, I'm not suggesting that an outlandish name for your business is the key to generating increased exposure. But I am strongly urging you to be creative when you think about advertising.

I do not think advertising is absolutely essential for your startup or growing business. You can often better use your limited budget for marketing on submarine sandwiches than ads. But as your business grows, advertising can be an effective component of your marketing endeavors, especially when there are opportunities to expose your business to mass audiences for free. For example, you could define your business and your employees on the well-known Wikipedia Internet site. You can also post videos on YouTube, open a Facebook or MySpace account and utilize other Internet and social networking opportunities. You may also serve as a news media source by writing letters to local newspapers, magazines or industry journals or calling radio and television stations to provide the media outlets with your "expert" opinions on topics that are important at a particular time.

When you have discretionary income, it may be time to advertise. But don't waste money on stale advertising tactics. Think outside the box; push the envelope; and be creative.

One of my best friends in the insurance industry is Mark Vitali, who has built a huge agency in North Carolina. Mark grew up in a lower middle-class neighborhood in upstate New York, played football at a small school called American International College and then finished his degree in a New York state school called Oswego. He actually began a career in the insurance business as a result of a significant car accident in 1992. "I fought with my workers compensation carrier and went to work for Nationwide in 1993 on the notion that if I couldn't beat them, then I would join them," Vitali said. He started from scratch and has built his business in excess of $25 million in premiums at the time of this writing. He is an absolute giant in North Carolina, the king, so to speak.

As such, Vitali uses a king in his commercials. "I now dedicate between ten to fifteen percent of my total budget on advertising," he said. "But before you do any advertising, you've got to find your target market. Many people think that advertising is all on TV but there are many mediums. I use

TV, but I'm very particular on how I use it. I have great TV commercials that are funny, and they have something inside of them that makes people look at them. In my case, I have a big man who is about 6-foot-4 and weighs about 400 pounds; he wears a king suit since we're the king of auto insurance. You've got to have something to catch the customer's eyes. We also have a dog in there because people love animals. We use the king and the dog in most—if not all—of our commercials. And if we're talking about insurance for young drivers, I have local teenagers in my ads. It's amazing how an entire school will watch that one kid. You have to have a catch, something that people will remember you by. Along those lines, we also have made a marketing impact by going to the high schools and asking if we can speak to classes about the cost of insurance. The schools have tended to let us do that when we tie it in with the affects of drinking and driving. My message was about money, but the true message was about not drinking and driving, and this is why it's going to cost you a fortune if you do it. Ultimately, it's getting the idea across that you've got to have insurance and the principal's generally love the message because it incorporates the dangers of drinking and driving. Part of the reason that I have had so much luck in opening those doors is probably because my commercials are so well received in the area. You need to do things that are different to be memorable."

You also need to remember to have a budget strategy. Mark Vitali can now afford to do whatever he wants from a marketing and advertising standpoint. But it wasn't always that way for him, and it won't be that way for you starting off. So, be creative with your marketing and advertising concepts... and how you pay for them. And as a general rule of thumb, never pay full price for your advertising.

It's difficult to generate much free media attention in the insurance industry. If you were doing a presentation to a school—as Mark has done—you could call the local newspapers and hopefully attract a reporter to the presentation or send a letter to the editor about the event.

Regardless of whether you can generate free publicity, you can always do it on a discount. As your business grows, advertising can be an important component of your overall marketing plan. But don't just buy ad space or television time without exploring all your options. You can receive 110 percent of the benefits of advertising by paying as little as 25 percent of the cost.

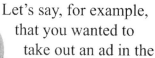

Let's say, for example, that you wanted to take out an ad in the local newspaper. Here again, I'm going to use an insurance example. But it can apply to any business. Most manufacturers, franchisors and distributors have co-op dollars available for promoting their products and services. The federal government also has numerous programs for various industries to promote consumer awareness.

CALL FOR CASH

Let's take flood insurance, for example. Most agents would simply call the local newspaper, find out the advertising rate for a quarter-page ad and send a check to the paper. That's a waste of your hard-earned money.

There is money to use to offset your costs if you are simply willing to make a few phone calls. The National Flood Insurance Program (NFIP) is more than willing to give you up to 75 percent of the total cost of your advertisement if you include their message. In other words, you put your corporate logo and contact information on the ad and include the NFIP message, and your $10,000 ad now costs you $2,500 to run. That's called cooperative—or co-op—advertising, and it is available for virtually any type of advertising. All the insurance companies have some type of cooperative advertising, but most agents simply don't take advantage of it. If you are going to be pushing Hartford life insurance, call Hartford and see how much they will contribute toward your ad. You will have to do some paperwork, but you will be reimbursed handsomely for your efforts. The same applies to Nationwide, Allstate, manufacturers, and franchisors.

The other thing people don't realize is that toward the end of the year, if you'll call a particular company in your industry, you may receive 100 percent reimbursement. Let's say that NFIP estimated that it was going to use $1 million for cooperative advertisement this calendar year, divided among each agent who applies for the cooperative agreement. The original plan may have been to reimburse each agent $10,000 per advertisement. But at the end of the year, there is often a surplus in the budget, because I would guesstimate that only about 5 percent of agents actually take the time to take advantage of the cooperative deals. Trust me. The money is available. And at the end of the year, company employees will practically be begging you to take the cooperative money so that their budget will increase or stay the same next year. I cannot stress enough how easy this money is to come by if you simply make the contacts and follow through.

Cooperative dollars can easily give your business a big-time presence. But forming partnerships isn't limited to advertising. Partnerships can also impact your marketing efforts in other ways. For example, one of my agents in Arlington, Texas called me and said he had a deal where he could gain access to a suite at the Ballpark in Arlington (home of the Texas Rangers) for two games for $5,000. That was more than I was willing to spend. But instead of telling him, "no," I wrote a proposal and sent it to an insurance company and the executives of the company said that they would split it with us. The company contributed $2,500, allowing my agent to take ten of his best clients to the suite for the baseball games. If I had been turned down, I would have found another business to go in for half the price. It doesn't even have to be someone tied to our business. You just have to talk to people. And in order to do that, you must have contacts.

If you want to get in the community newspaper when you're first starting off to let people know that you are in business, the more ads you buy, the cheaper the advertising space will be. So, why not partner with a contact who is in a totally different business? Perhaps an accountant you met at a Chamber of Commerce breakfast. Maybe a lawyer you met at a networking function. Whatever the case, you can buy a year's worth of advertising and split it up to receive 26 weeks for each of you. By going this route, your advertising rate is much cheaper because you and your partner bought all 52 weeks of the year instead of buying 26 ads.

Be courageous; be creative; and be active in your marketing efforts. It should not cost you an arm and a leg to market your business. You should also not be intimidated to market yourself. You can build your business with a box of donuts or a couple of submarine sandwiches. You can advertise for pennies on the dollar. You can make all the contacts you need by attending the next party you receive an invitation to—and spending 80 percent of your time at the party meeting the people in the room that you do not know. Marketing is not rocket science; it's common sense. If you possess—or can develop—some ordinary social skills, you can build an extraordinary business.

GAME DAY PREP

1. What's the most cost-effective form of marketing and advertising?

   A. Putting your face (or other body parts) on the reverse side of the kiddie seat of shopping carts at the grocery store.

   B. Placing a full-page color ad in the Swimsuit edition of Sports Illustrated.

   C. Renting the Goodyear Blimp and flying your company logo during the World Series and the Super Bowl.

   D. None of the above. Be much more creative and fiscally responsible than that.

   Answer here _____

2. It's your restaurant's grand opening weekend. To drive customers to your establishment in the most cost-effective manner you should:

   A. Spend tens of thousands of dollars mailing out coupons.

   B. Take out a billboard on the nearest interstate.

   C. Actively pursue the employees of the businesses in your area by taking a plate of your best appetizers to various businesses with a buy one, get one free coupon.

   D. Dress up as a clown and wave at traffic as it goes by. Provide the middle finger to those who do not stop.

   Answer here _____

3. When building relationships with centers of influence to solicit referred leads to your company, you should:

   A. Ask not what your company can do for them, but what their company can do for you.

B. Beg the person of influence for a referral.

C. Build a partnership that mutually benefits their company and your company.

D. Cater a fine meal and leave a huge stack of business cards next to the break room trash can.

Answer here_____

More detailed information about the topics covered in this chapter is available at www.gameplanbook.com.

The website is continually updated to provide the latest information, forms, instructions and tips to help you build or grow your business.

Extra Points - Notes

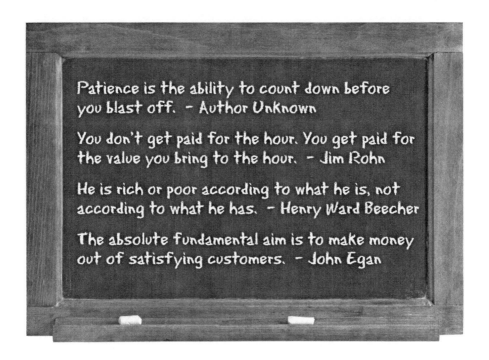

Patience is the ability to count down before you blast off. - Author Unknown

You don't get paid for the hour. You get paid for the value you bring to the hour. - Jim Rohn

He is rich or poor according to what he is, not according to what he has. - Henry Ward Beecher

The absolute fundamental aim is to make money out of satisfying customers. - John Egan

CHAPTER 4

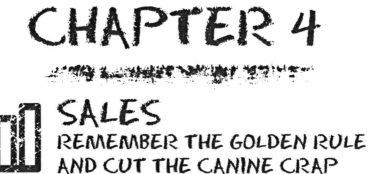

SALES
REMEMBER THE GOLDEN RULE AND CUT THE CANINE CRAP

Before you skip this chapter on sales because you think your in the lawn business, dry cleaning business, consulting business,... **everyone, I mean everyone** is in the sales business. If you can't sell your ideas as an accountant, attorney or businessowner...you will not be successful. So read this chapter on sales!

81

According to the editor of a "Dog Owner's Guide," there are at least 60 million dogs living in roughly 37 million households across the United States. I emphasize the words "at least" because those numbers only apply to dog owners who regularly take their canines to the vet. There are probably millions of other dogs in the United States, and since one of those dogs resides in my own home, I suppose you could consider us a dog family. In fact, I even risked life and limb one day to rescue my dog from coyotes, but that's another story.

The point here is that many Americans are absolutely fanatical about their four-legged friends, which would explain why the American Pet Products Manufacturers Association has forecasted that pet owners will spend more than $50 billion in pet supplies by the year 2010. That's an awful lot of dog food, chew toys and pooper-scoopers.

That $50 billion figure piqued my business interests, and I began to wonder why we are so willing to spend so much money on our animals. I'm not talking about purchasing necessities like food or heart-worm preventatives; I'm talking about the ridiculous doggie sweaters and the frivolous fur-ball items that scream, "Excess!" You can, for example, purchase a "Furcedes Car Dog Bed" for $350 at GlamourDog and you can buy a Colonial Mansion Dog House from The Well Appointed House for a mere $6,160. I'm not making this up. Most dogs I have been around would rather roll in their own feces than sleep in a Furcedes, but many Americans will do almost anything to pamper their pooch. Why?

The obvious reason is that many dogs become part of the families where they reside. But we can also learn plenty about how to live our lives from our dogs. I recently read a list titled, "What we learn from our dogs." It included points such as: "Love unconditionally; when loved ones come home, run to greet them; never pass up an opportunity to go for a joy ride; never pretend to be something you're not; run, romp and play daily; drink lots of water; and avoid biting when a simple growl will suffice."

All good points. As far as I'm concerned, though, we can also learn quite a bit about becoming good salespeople from observing our canines. In terms of following your dog's positive traits as a salesperson, you should sniff out all of your good leads; you should trust your senses; and you should bound out the door each and every day with vigor and enthusiasm. But here's the most important sales lesson of all you can learn from watching a dog—and it's not a positive trait: Don't beg. Never, ever. Whether you are selling incense or insurance; widgets or Winnebagos, you never want to be perceived as being desperate. I'm going to be very straightforward and blunt here. In my observations of countless salespeople through the years, I see far too many people who act like humping dogs toward their prospects. They basically attack their prospects, use them, offend them and keep coming back for more even when they are pushed away. The prospect usually feels more violated than motivated to buy.

You will not make many sales in any industry utilizing the full, frontal attack mode. Nor will you keep many customers by continually lunging at them, jumping on them or pestering them. I've seen sales

OFFER

forces act like a pack of wild dogs, trampling through neighborhoods or subdivisions with reckless abandon; I've seen salespeople who operate in constant pounce mode; and I've heard the non-stop begging of salespeople who regularly find themselves barking up the wrong tree. Quite frankly, they all need to be sent to obedience school.

Truly effective salespeople have learned the difference between offering a product or service and attempting to force it down someone's throat. They know when to ask for a prospect's business and when to back away. They know how to handle objections without being confrontational. And they know that one of the most important rules to being a good salesperson is to be a good person. "The Golden Rule" should not merely apply to your spiritual or personal life. It should also be applied to your sales approach. In the New Testament (Matthew 7:12), Jesus sums up the Golden Rule by saying "Do unto others as you would have them do unto you." There are also references to this same fundamental principle in the Old Testament, Confucianism, Buddhism, Islam, Hinduism and virtually every other religious doctrine. It is also expressed by Homer in The Odyssey.

It is so prevalent throughout recorded history because it is such an important principle to our overall quality of life; to the health of our relationships; to the conduct of our communities; and to our society as a whole. So, why do so many salespeople think that this rule shouldn't apply to their profession? And why do so many salespeople replace this fundamental truth with techniques such as fast-talking, high pressure, scare tactics, etc.?

The key to effective sales and customer retention is practicing the

Golden Rule. I've been to hundreds of conferences and read thousands of articles and books preaching theories about the secrets and magic words of sales. Practically everyone has heard the "feel, felt, found" technique that goes like this, "I know how you feel; I felt the same way; but this is what I found…" I'm also well-versed in the "do not give them an option to put you off strategy," which goes something like, "Would it be better to meet at 2 p.m. or 4 p.m. or on Wednesday or Thursday?" Then there's the "answer every question with a question" philosophy and the "this deal is good for today only" technique. And, of course, there's the old bait and switch technique.

All of those techniques—and many other trivial ones—turn me off quicker than a cold shower. In my opinion—and in many years of experience—there are no magic words, formulas or phrases in sales. If you want to generate great sales numbers, be genuine. The integrity of your words is far more important than the speed or smooth nature of your conversations. Think candor, not catch-phrases. Be sincere, not slick. Be passionate, but don't resort to pressure. And always keep the Golden Rule in mind, asking yourself, "How would I like to be approached or presented if it was me on the other end of this call/conversation?"

Obviously, there have been volumes of books written about sales. But I am completely convinced that the Golden Rule theory is the summation of every book, every article, every seminar and every lecture I have ever read, listened to or watched. You do not need a doctorate in psychology or a master's in marketing to be a highly effective salesperson. What you need is a little common sense, a lot of persistence, some patience and a few tricks of the trade that can turn you into a top dog—the leader of the sales pack—and distance you from the flea bags, mutts and tramps in the sales industry who wander the streets aimlessly, treating every day as hump day…if you get my drift.

PRACTICE BEFORE YOU PREACH

As I have mentioned previously, forget the magic words when talking to prospects. Be yourself, be genuine, be honest...but don't be unprepared, either. It's a good thing if your sales pitch is not predictable, stale and filled with more clichés than a football coach's postgame press conference. But you also need to practice your sales pitch to handle any objections. Practice with your spouse, practice with your kids, practice with your neighbors and practice in front of the mirror. And don't stop practicing after you've made a few sales.

Can you imagine Tiger Woods going into a tournament without practicing? Can you imagine him not practicing just because he has won on the PGA Tour before? Of course not. Woods has a beautiful golf swing because he practices it on a daily basis. He knows he is capable of swinging the club perfectly, hitting one drive after another in the fairway, chipping onto every green and draining virtually every putt. He's the world's best golfer, after all. So, why does he practice daily, standing out in the rain, the cold, the intense heat—whatever the conditions—to work on a swing that is already the picture of perfection? Woods understands that every day, every new round and every new course present new challenges. He also understands that if he doesn't devote time each week to staying on top of his game, he will eventually slip. So, Woods practices his game on the driving range; he works on shots out of the rough; he hits wedges out of the sand trap; he putts from various distances. He receives the instant feedback from how well he drives the ball and how close his approach shots land near the cup, and he also has a swing coach who can help him decipher any flaws in his game that might arise. That's what it takes for Woods to rise to the top and stay there.

PRACTICE

Same with the great hitters in baseball. It has always been rather amazing to me that the greatest hitters in the game—guys like Tony Gwynn, Wade Boggs, Rod Carew, etc.—all utilized a batting tee in their daily routine. These guys all proved that they could hit a fastball at 90 mph or slap a curveball into the gap. You might think  that they would have no need for a tee, because they hit a moving object with such consistency. But the best of the best chose to start their day by hitting off a stationary tee. Why? Because they understood that the basics of their swing needed to be practiced on a daily basis. If you perfect your swing on a tee, your muscle memory will take over in a game. The more you practice, the better your skills become; the better your skills are, the more you get paid. Athletes obviously understand this concept.

The same principles can—and should—be applied to sales or any other business. I'm not necessarily suggesting that you need to practice your sales pitch every day. But if your spouse lobs you a few softball objections each week, you are more likely to be ready for a prospect's curveballs. Practice before you preach. And be prepared for all possible objections.

Allow me to give you an example from my own line of work. I am not suggesting that you memorize my words. On the contrary, I think you should tailor it to your own personality and your prospect's personal preferences. But regardless of what you're selling, I believe there will come a time when a prospect will bring up the price objection. The objection may go something like this, Warren, the policy looks good, but I think I can get cheaper premiums at ABC Insurance Company down the street. I think I will go with them, instead."

Now, it should be strongly noted here that most people really don't buy on price alone. If that were truly the case, everyone on the planet would be shopping at Wal-Mart, driving a Kia, living in cookie-cutter homes, drinking Pabst Blue Ribbon beer, celebrating special occasions at McDonald's and wearing no-name clothing lines. You know differently, of course. So, let me handle the price objection with something like this:

"Joe, I commend you for being wise with your money, and I understand what you're saying about the price of our policy. But throughout my life I've discovered that people are generally looking for three things when they come to buy a product or service. They are looking for the lowest possible price, the highest quality product, and the best service. Can you name one company in our country that is a leader in all three of those categories—low price, high service, and high quality? Let's use Wal-Mart as an example. They are a leader in lowest price. But how about highest service and highest quality? Have you ever returned something at Wal-Mart? If you have, it was probably a lengthy, frustrating experience, huh?

"Now, have you ever returned something at Neiman Marcus? I have. My wife bought a purse at Neiman Marcus and it broke four times. When I took it back in, they didn't say, 'Can I see a receipt?' They said, 'Mr. Barhorst, we'll take care of that for you; it would be our pleasure.'

"Admittedly, considering the cost, we probably bought four purses when we bought it the first time. But you see my point. In any business, you can't be the leader in all three categories. Zig Ziglar may have said it best with this quote: "The common law of business balance prohibits paying a little and getting a lot; it can't be done."

In other words, you get what you pay for. You can't offer the cheapest rates and also provide the highest quality products and the best service, because it takes paying qualified people competitive salaries to truly deliver great products and services. So, when you look at insuring your home, which one do you want to give up? Price, quality product or service? If you say service, I can't provide less services to you. Our standards are world-class service, and we provide that to all of our customers whether they buy one policy or 10 policies from us. I can change features of our product; I can raise the deductible; I can remove coverage; and I can do all kinds of things to reduce the quality of your policy, which will lower the price. But doing that may ultimately cost you much more than you are saving if you have a claim and the damage is not covered."

I didn't just come up with that off the top of my head. Nor did I merely shoot from the hip. I practiced it; I acted it out in front of the mirror; I rehearsed it with my wife. So, when the objection was raised, I was prepared to handle it. I didn't beg; I didn't use any fancy language; I didn't resort to scare tactics. Yes, I mentioned reducing coverage, but I didn't go into great detail about losing his home, the devastation of not having all of your assets and family memories protected, etc. It's not my intent to scare someone into buying a policy from me; nor is it my intent to dazzle them with flowery language. My intent is to handle the objection without being caught off guard. The problem with many salespeople is that they don't practice a way to overcome price objections. You must if you are going to have long-term success.

Another strategy I might use with someone who raises price as an objection is what I call the gasoline principle. Drive down any busy street or pull up to a busy intersection, and there's a good chance that you will see several different gas stations. Let's use Exxon and Shell as examples here. I've always wondered how Exxon can have its gasoline priced three cents cheaper than Shell can some weeks, and then Shell is cheaper two weeks later. They go back and forth. From a business perspective, it has caused me to ponder because neither brand has a drilling technology advantage that would allow it to pull oil out of the ground cheaper; neither has a dramatically different processing technology or a refining technology that can make their gas any cheaper. Both corporations advertise on television; they both sponsor events; they both have high towers full of executives and marketing people. So, why is Exxon cheaper than Shell this week? And why was Shell cheaper than Exxon last week?

It's a marketing game, where each gas station is trying to get customers to come into the station and look at their store. They are trying to sell coffee or donuts. They are trying to lure people into the store to make money on what's inside the store, non-essential products such as newspapers, lottery tickets, etc. So, they will lower the price of gas for a week or two to get people to come in and see the coffee variety or the cleanliness of their restrooms. Then the price will go back up or the competitor on the other corner will lower its prices. But I think what you would find if you stuck with Shell or Exxon over an extended period, you would probably pay the same amount of money because neither one of them has a technological or price advantage. So, if price was an objection with a prospect, I would go through the gasoline example and relate it to my business. Here's what I would say: "Like the gas stations, insurance companies are similar in the marketing game they play. State Farm insures houses in your neighborhood; Nationwide insures houses in your neighborhood; so does Traveler's and so do many other companies. But we're all subject to the same hail storms; we're all subject to the same statistics for fire; we're all in the same neighborhood for hurricanes. Our exposure is the same. Our risk to loss is the same. If you looked inside the home offices of all of these companies, they've got ivory towers for the executives; they've got big marketing departments; they have huge overhead costs. They are all basically the same. So if you took two or three of the major carriers and compared the price of your insurance over the course of your lifetime, there probably wouldn't be a two or three percent difference among the three of them. So, my point to you, as a consumer, is that you probably should buy a policy from the individual agent who provides the best service, not from the carrier that features this week's lowest price."

Here again, I believe I have handled the objection logically and deductively. I haven't resorted to high-pressure tactics; I haven't said anything about this being a one-time offer. And perhaps most significantly, I have pointed out that selling insurance—or automobiles, accounting services, homes, property or virtually anything else—comes down to relationships. In my business, I want to be known as the insurance guy. Plain and simple. That's who I want to be known as when I take my kids to the Little League ballpark; that's who I want to be known as when I take my wife to the movie theater; that's who I want to be known as when I go to church. If I become that—and if I treat people right—they will eventually come to me for their insurance needs and insurance questions because of the relationship we have, which takes me back to the "Golden Rule" principle we discussed earlier in this chapter. It also takes me back to the dog theory we discussed earlier.

You are not going to sell any policies or any sports cars at church. You're not going to close a home mortgage at a neighborhood barbecue. So, don't try to do it then. Treat people with respect, tell them what you do, and they will eventually come to you or you can eventually call on them. But the relationship must be built first. I cannot stress this point enough. I've seen guys on their honeymoon, sitting next to their bikini-clad bride, trying to sell their product on the beach to a stranger they bumped into in the hotel lobby. My assessment of this person: Humping dog. I've also seen salespeople at their kids' dance recital, ignoring the performance of their daughters on stage so that they can try to sell a condo to the person sitting next to them. Wrong approach. Wrong timing. If I am the prospect sitting next to this salesperson—even if I am in the market for a condo—I'm thinking two things: 1. Humping dog. 2. Shut up!

It's great to meet new people; it's essential to develop new contacts; and you must become comfortable with working a room. But patience and perspective are vital. Sometimes you've got 30 seconds to make a first impression; sometimes you've got three seconds. Your goal in meeting new people should be to make a new friend, not to make a new sale. If you do that, you are likely to make a good first impression. If you don't do that, you may never get a second chance to meet with that person. It takes a long time to recover from a bad first impression.

With that said, I must warn you that if you are going to be a great salesperson, you must be aware of the fact that you are essentially on the clock 24 hours a day, seven days a week, 365 days a year. That can be a blessing or a burden. You never know when people are going to be observing you; you never know when you are going to bump into someone who could be a potential prospect; and you always must be aware of the fact that when you go out of the house on any day of the week and at practically any time of the day, you may have a chance to make a first impression—good or bad. I've seen salespeople ruin  their reputation by making a scene at the Little League ballpark. If you have the desire, ability and time to coach your son's youth baseball team, that's great. But if the umpire makes a poor call, be aware that all of your team's parents and all of the other team's parents will be watching you to see how you handle that bad call, how you deal with the umpire and how you set an example for the kids. You also need to be aware of how you treat department store salespeople, how you treat the waitress or waiter, how you act at your spouse's company Christmas party, how much alcohol you consume in a public setting, etc. You want to be known as the "Insurance Guy" or the "Mortgage Guy" or the "Financial Planner Person." You do not want to be known as the hot-head, the jerk, the drunk, the cheap-tipper. Remember the Golden Rule, and you will be fine. But it takes time to build a good reputation, while one can be lost in a matter of seconds.

And even the most innocent expeditions outside the house can help make or break you in terms of finding potential prospects. I remember, for example, when Lisa and I first started our business, and we didn't have a dime to spare. An associate who had an office in the same strip center as me had a 1983 Toyota Celica Supra for sale. The car was 10 years old when I bought it from him, and it featured four flat tires. I cleaned it up and managed to get it running so it would look presentable enough where I could make sales calls in that car. Business eventually began to pick up, and I began to make plans to buy a new car and sell the Supra. So, I loaded up my three-year-old son and drove to a carwash, where I even sprayed down the engine to give it a new shine. Unfortunately, all the grease that was on the engine washed into the exhaust system, and the car caught on fire on the way home. Now, remember that I was coming back from the carwash, so I was wearing ragged—and very short-shorts—with no shirt. When my car caught on fire, I pulled over immediately, grabbed my son and ran up to a house on the route back to my own home. I knocked on the door and asked to use a water hose. I also asked the woman who answered the door if she could watch my son while I tried and put the fire out. Well, as it turned out, the couple that lived in that house also went to our church. I assure you that they never looked at me as the Insurance Guy when they saw me at church. On the contrary, they probably looked at me as the greasy, shirtless lunatic who endangered his own son by driving a car that blew up in front of their house. Or, at best, they looked at me as the idiot who didn't know enough about cars to be more careful washing down his engine.

Maybe that's not fair. After all, everybody's entitled to mistakes, right? I did nothing immoral or illegal. But perception is reality, and this couple's initial perception of me was poor...at best. I'm not sure if I would have ever sold that couple a policy under any circumstances. But I do know that I blew any chance to make a strong first impression with them.

That may seem inconsequential. It's not. As salespeople, our goal should be to make a good, strong first impression with everyone we meet. Is that possible? No. Different people have different personalities, and it is impossible to strike a connection with everyone you meet. In fact, there will be many people you will meet who you will have no desire to work with, regardless of how profitable it could be for you.

Nevertheless, the goal for all salespeople should be to make a strong first impression, to start a conversation, to develop some kind of personal relationship. It may take years for you to make a sale to that person; and it may never happen. But eventually, the ultimate goal from a sales perspective is to be viewed by that person in such a positive light that he or she comes to you with questions. Rarely have I ever asked one of my friends, family members, associates, neighbors, fellow church members, etc. to purchase an insurance policy from me. In fact, the secret to my success as a salesperson is that I spend very little time involved in what most people would consider "sales mode." Marketing mode, yes. Relationship-building approach, absolutely. But selling? Asking for business? Not unless the time is absolutely right.

My neighbors know me as the "Insurance Guy." So do my friends at the gym and at church. They know what I do, and they also know that I have never pushed a policy on them. They've watched me; they've grown to trust me; and they've learned that they can come to me with insurance questions. But even when they ask me a question at church, in the front yard or at the gym, I don't leap at them and whip out a contract. I answer their questions, I listen to their personal situations, and I offer them advice. This is how I would want to be treated.

If I discovered that my workout partner owned an auto repair shop and I had some questions about how my car was running. If he immediately put the hard sell on me about coming into his shop, I'd think, "Humping dog." All I did was ask him a question about his area of expertise. Think back to the Golden Rule theory again. How would you want to be treated in a similar situation?

Just trust me here. If you treat people with respect, I have found that when they are in the market for insurance, they will come to me. They will come to my office. They will call me and ask me if I can help them. That's the time to make a sales presentation; that's the time to handle objections with the pitch you have practiced; and that's the time to ask them for their business. Not before then. If you do it before then—when they don't have a need—it's often a waste of time and a lost prospect.

Depending on where you are in your sales career right now, I can probably predict what you are thinking at this instant. If you are just starting off, you are probably thinking that I'm nuts. In fact, you're probably mumbling something like: "Hey Warren, I just opened my business. I don't have the time to spend years or even months developing a relationship. I need to make some sales. I need income. Immediately."

I know where you are coming from. But you can build relationships while at the same time building your business. You can also make cold calls without coming across as the desperate, humping dog. And you can market your business without coming across as pushy, annoying, aggressive or desperate.

IMPRESSIONS

I've covered various marketing techniques in the previous chapter, but let me give you another brief example of how I might proactively market without being pushy. I might walk into a business I'm pitching, and say we've got a great program for dry cleaners. We just took care of (or just presented the opportunity to) Bill Smith down the street and showed him how to save some money by rearranging his coverage. I'd love to get your opinion on this plan, and I was just wondering if it would be something you were interested in reviewing?

I didn't say, "I've got something for you." I didn't say, "I've got a deal for you." I soft-sold it. He may still say, "Get the hell outta my store." But more than likely, he'll take a look at what I'm offering because his competitor, Bill Smith, took a look at it and/or I asked him to give me his opinion on it. That is how I would cold call or start the particular conversation. And if I was going to go out to make a direct call, I'd slow play it so that I would not be perceived as the humping dog.

One final word of advice on not being desperate: DO NOT say "yes" to everything. When you are on the verge of making a sale, you certainly want to be accommodating. You want to fulfill as many requests as possible. But you do not want to be so desperate to finalize the sale that you lose money on it, waste too much time on it or ruin your career because of it. You need to know exactly what you are capable of doing before agreeing to a potential buyer's requests, and you need to be willing to say, "no," or "I simply cannot handle that," or "I don't know the answer to that, but I can get back to you?" Remember: Always under-promise and over-deliver.

Here again, you have to take yourself and your own desires

out of the equation. You have to truly look at what is best for the prospect and answer accordingly. If you're doing what is best for you, you're probably not going to be successful. It's perfectly acceptable—even quite beneficial to your long term relationship with that prospect—to tell a client, "We don't have a solution for you. You need to stay with the carrier you are with; it's a better value than what I have for you." If you say something like that, you just earned the client's ultimate respect. He or she will come back to you for other needs, and he or she will certainly refer others to you.

You also need to be willing to say to yourself, "This project is simply too big for me." You shouldn't even present an opportunity to someone when you know it will stretch you too thin. For example, if you're in the restaurant business, but your specialty is submarine sandwiches, you probably shouldn't try to cater black-tie formal events—even though you are technically in the restaurant business. It's a recipe for disaster. For me personally, I would love to be big enough and well-rounded enough to handle the 401K plan for every employee at a huge department store chain or a major university like Texas A&M. But I simply do not have the infrastructure in place to handle something like that. I wouldn't present that plan, and even if it was offered to me, I would turn it down, saying something like, "I am really honored that you would think of me to do that, but we just don't have the scale and capacity to put that together. If it's something you really want me to do, I could explore the costs, but it would take us two years to put the people in place to do that."

Now, I know many salespeople who would say, "Hell, yes," and worry about the consequences later. But it's a big mistake that can literally ruin your company and your career. It's great to stretch, but not so far that it breaks your business.

When I was in the crane business, I was trying to sell some equipment to a major airline company and it was a couple of million dollar project. We were really the only crane manufacturer with the financial capabilities to build the project. But another company in Houston, which had a very poor financial rating, made a bid that was much lower than our bid. The airline went with the other company's bid, although we went back to the airline and told them that they were making a mistake. "You're going to bankrupt that company," we said. That company had no chance of actually living up to its end of the bid, and guess who finished building those cranes? The airline purchased that company, finished its own project and sold off the assets of the company because it went bankrupt attempting to handle a deal that was simply too big for it to handle. The crane company was desperate to get the deal, and it got it. But it also went right out of business. Don't bite off more than you can chew.

SETTING UP THE DEAL PROACTIVELY FOR AN EASY CLOSE

I have obviously spent a great deal of time discussing how to set up prospects, the importance of building a relationship with prospects, how to handle objections and how to treat clients with the Golden Rule approach. The final step in the sales equation does, indeed, involve actually closing the deal. I have saved this item for last because it is the most important step in the process. But here again, the Golden Rule applies.

For the most part, the time to make a sale is when the client comes to or calls your office, invites you to his home or office and has decided that he wants to do business with you. At this stage, you have built some kind of relationship; you have developed some trust; and you have probably already handled some objections. But even at this stage in the sales game, you do not want to go for the kill. I've seen many salespeople blow the deal at the final stage because their own adrenaline gets the best of them. Too many salespeople stop conversing and start attempting to conquer their clients at this stage; they become as aggressive as sharks who have smelled blood in the water. Show a little patience; show some restraint; show some respect and you will close most deals without any problem.

In my personal approach to this stage, we have developed something called the Proactive Service Experience (PSE). This is designed to inform our prospective clients exactly what we will do for them as their insurance agency. Our sales process is much more than just providing a price quote for their insurance. That's not a proactive approach. Sure we provide a quote and a proposal, but we also lay everything else out on the table for the client so they can make a fully informed decision.

This PSE approach can be adapted to any industry or any-sized agency. For sake of example, however, I am going to walk through the Proactive Service Experience from our operation. Let's assume Joe and Betty Smith are not my clients, and something has changed

in their lives (new home, new car, birth of a child, new job, etc.) to make them pick up the phone and call me. Remember, I have positioned myself so that Joe and Betty have come to know me as the Insurance Guy; they have not done business with me in the past, but I am one of the agents that they have decided to call to get a price on their new insurance needs.

Hopefully, Joe and Betty will call another office first, and the agent will ask them if they have a copy of their renewal page, their declarations page or their bill. The agent asks Joe and Betty to fax a copy of it to the office, so that agency can perform an apples-to-apples comparison to provide them a quote. Joe and Betty fax it over and the agent copies all of the existing coverage, and inputs it into the system, gets a price, crosses his fingers and then prays or hopes that his agency has a lower price than what Joe and Betty currently have with their insurance provider. That's the standard, non-proactive approach, and that is how most inexperienced salespeople think products are sold. But what really has happened is that this agent has copied all the mistakes that the last guy made when Joe and Betty bought insurance. This is a prescription without diagnosis, and it should be considered malpractice. This type of example is rampant in the insurance industry and most other industries, as well. Salespeople fail to realize that they should be teachers and consultants, not order takers.

What really needs to happen in any sales process—and especially in the insurance sales process—is to have a conversation with Joe and Betty about their life and their personal situation. In order for me to provide them with a truly accurate insurance solution and to take price out as an objection, I must follow this process. I'm rarely ever going to provide an apples-to-apples comparison because what Joe and Betty have right now is probably not what they're going to need. My job as their agent is to educate and illustrate to them all of the risks and exposures they currently have, provide an insurance solution or recommendation, and then it becomes Joe and Betty's decision to purchase policies to cover what is most important to them.

In the beginning of my conversation, I'm going to tell Joe and Betty how the insurance industry works. I am going to explain how other agencies copy the old policy and hope that they have the lowest price. I am going to tell them that the reason they are buying the insurance is to make sure that it covers them in their time of need. I am going to tell them that we are different. This will help me build or reinforce the relationship I have with them and further enhance the level of trust they have in me. Then I'm going to tell Joe and Betty what happens if they buy a policy from the Barhorst Insurance Group—this is the Proactive Service Experience which is our differentiation strategy. It is about a three-minute conversation on what you receive if you become our client.

Most salespeople fail to capitalize on this valuable part of the sales process. They are so hungry for the kill of the sale that they try to rush the process. In essence, our PSE is simply this: "Joe and Betty, when you become a client of the Barhorst Insurance Group

we promise to explain what the policy covers in terms you can understand; we explain how the billing process works; we explain what you should do if you have a claim; we completely explain what you should do if you need to service your policy and explain replacement cost and the inspection process. We're not going to hide anything, we want to be your advocate."

Then we will say: "Joe and Betty, here's what we are going to do after you become a client: We're going to do the work for you by contacting your mortgage company, canceling your current policy and notifying your lien holder. Two to three weeks from now, we are also going to call you to make sure you have received your policy and everything is correct. And throughout the year we will place a follow-up call to notify you if your policy cancels or is in "warned" status for nonpayment. We'll place a follow-up call if you have filed a claim to ensure that process is being handled in a timely fashion; we'll review your account each time we have contact with you; and we will place an annual review call 30 to 60 days before your policy renews to thank you for your business and offer you an account review."

Many agents and agencies do these exact same things.

Thank You !

But they fail to let the client know in advance what the process is and how the agency is working for the client throughout the year. They miss a golden opportunity to provide a Golden Rule presentation. After I take prospects through the PSE, the typical response is, "Man, you guys really have it going on."

We have built our agency on these fundamental behaviors and business tactics. With this method, we not only sell numerous policies, we also recover potential lost business. If your bill is late, you will receive a phone call from us that might go something like this: "Hey Joe and Betty, this is Warren, and we've noticed that we haven't received your payment for April. Just wanted to make sure it has not been lost in the mail."

PSE

Before the Sale	After the Sale		Throughout the Year		
Explain	We do the Work	Follow-Up Call	Cancellation Notice/Late Pay Call Claims Follow-Up Call Review Account	Annual Review	Account Completion

In today's busy world most clients are very thankful of this call. If Joe and Betty tell me they have switched providers, I have an opportunity to save that policy. So we call people with late bills. Always have. Always will. Many executives and industry consultants would advise agents to never call on late bills because you are setting a precedent that could cause an "errors and omission" claim. The customer could claim that he/she didn't pay a bill because we didn't contact them this particular month. But my objective—in all cases—is long-term relationships with my customers. We're not begging for table scraps; we're building relationships. After I cover the PSE it is then—and usually only then—that I make my insurance presentation and ask my client for his or her business.

Any business in any industry can create a proactive service experience to differentiate itself from its competitors. Don't assume your customers will see that you are different. You must tell them why and how you are different. It's a process that is rooted in building a relationship and treating prospects and clients with the Golden Rule approach. You can sell a policy, an automobile or virtually anything else with some fast-talking or high-pressure methods. But the money in the insurance industry is in renewals, and the money in any other industry comes from repeat customers and referrals. If that's what you're seeking—and it should be—take a look at your dog. Model his good behaviors and stay far away from his annoying traits.

GAME DAY PREP

1. The key to effective sales and customer retention is:
    A. Humping your prospect's leg like you are in heat.
    B. Practicing the Golden Rule approach and treating prospects the way you would like to be treated.
    C. Making sure you wear really short shorts and look totally unprofessional during meetings.
    D. Getting your prospects liquored up before you ask for their business.

    Answer here _____

2. The PSE (Proactive Service Experience) is designed to:
    A. Inform our prospective clients exactly what we will do for them as their business partner.
    B. Ward off PMS.
    C. Make our customers think we have a really fancy degree program.
    D. Make our customers think we are brokers associated with the Philippine Stock Exchange.

    Answer here _____

3. As an entrepreneur you should always, always say yes" to potential clients even if you know that you and your company will probably self-implode because the job you are being asked to do is way too big.
    A. True
    B. False

    Answer here _____

More detailed information about the topics covered in this chapter is available at www.gameplanbook.com.

The website is continually updated to provide the latest information, forms, instructions and tips to help you build or grow your business.

Extra Points - Notes

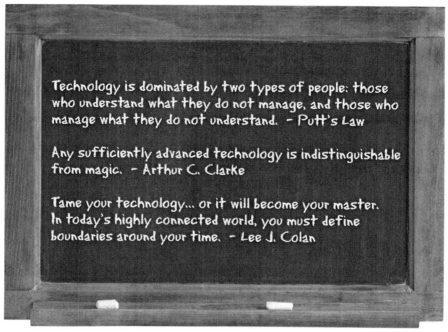

CHAPTER 5

LEVERAGING TECHNOLOGY

ONLY TO IMPROVE OR ENHANCE...

One of the most fascinating books of the Bible was written by the prophet Daniel in approximately 530 B.C. Jesus refers warmly to Daniel in the New Testament, and the man lived an absolutely incredible life. His life story is fascinating, but it's the last verses of the Book of Daniel that have always mesmerized me. In Daniel 12, for example, the prophet is seeing a vision from God regarding the "end times." Daniel is so overwhelmed by what he is seeing that he does not comprehend it all. When he questions the revelation he is receiving, Daniel is told (12:4) "But you, Daniel, close up and seal the words of the scroll until the time of the end. Many will go here and there to increase knowledge."

Let me quickly say that I am not enough of a Biblical expert to expound on whether or not we are living in the end times. Nor is it my goal in this setting to preach to you. But no matter your religious or faith-based beliefs, you've got to admit that, as Daniel predicted, we are living in some mind-boggling, knowledge-increasing times. And if you do not at least stay up with the technology advances and how they impact business, it could mark the "end times" for your career.

Just yesterday, it seems, I was playing a high-tech game called "Pong" with my fellow classmates while listening to my transistor radio or lugging around my "boom box." In college, I was using an electric typewriter—quite advanced for the time—and huge bottles

You've got what it takes to succeed.

of White Out. Then, when I went into the workplace, I wasted endless amounts of time hand-feeding a fax machine and waiting for a dial-up Internet connection to upload a simple document. If I needed to call someone on the road, I found a payphone. If I required information for a research project, I went to the library or found an Encyclopedia. If I needed to send someone a document, I bought stamps. If I needed a map, I went to a convenience store. If I needed to pay a bill or an employee, I wrote a check. If I wanted to shop for bargains, I searched the ads in the Sunday newspaper. And if I wanted to change the television channel, it wasn't that long ago that I had to actually get up off the couch and manually flip the dial.

My kids can hardly believe that I survived such hard-wired, snail-mail, analog-laden dark ages. They have never even heard of rabbit ears, rotary-dial phones, carbon copies, MS-DOS or "Mork and Mindy." What I find hard to believe, however, is how quickly times have changed. In the early to mid-1990s—hardly prehistoric times in my book—the World Wide Web was still far more of a novelty than a necessity. Cell phones were still primarily a luxury—and highly unreliable, at best. Blackberries were a fruit, scanning was performed almost exclusively by boys at the beach, and Google was a word known only to babbling toddlers.

My, oh my, how times and technology have changed. And in the words of that great musical prophet Bachman-Turner Overdrive— from the primeval ages of the 8-track cassette era—"You Ain't Seen Nothing Yet."

Karl Fisch, a high school technology teacher and world-renowned World Wide Web "blogger," put together an astounding PowerPoint presentation in 2006 called, *Did You Know?* It's a lengthy presentation, but here are some of the more interesting highlights— from a business perspective—that Fisch reported:

- "According to former Secretary of Education Richard Riley, the top 10 prospective in-demand jobs in the year 2010 did not exist in 2004.
- We are currently preparing students for jobs that don't yet exist, using technologies that haven't been invented in order to solve problems we don't even know are problems yet.
- There are over 2.7 billion searches performed on Google each month.
- The number of text messages sent and received every day exceeds the population of the planet.
- There are about 540,000 words in the English language, which is about five times as many as during

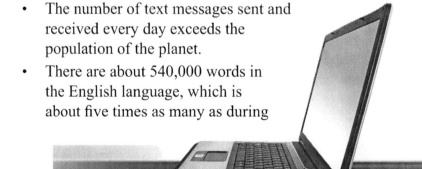

Shakespeare's time.

- More than 3,000 new books are published. . .daily.
- It's estimated that a week's worth of New York Times contains more information than a person was likely to come across in a lifetime in the 18th century.
- Approximately 40 exabytes (that's 4.0 x 1019) of unique new information was projected to be generated worldwide in 2007. That's estimated to be more than in the previous 5,000 years.
- The amount of new technical information is doubling every two years. It's predicted to double every 72 hours by 2010.
- Third-generation fiber optics has recently been separately tested by NEC and Alcatel that pushes 10 trillion bits per second down one strand of fiber. That's 1,900 CDs or 150 million simultaneous phone calls every second. It's currently tripling about every six months and is expected to do so for at least the next 20 years.
- 47 million laptops were shipped worldwide in 2006.
- Predictions are that by 2013 a supercomputer will be built that exceeds the computation capability of the human brain and by 2023, a $1,000 computer will exceed the computation capability of the human brain.
- Predictions are that by 2049 a $1,000 computer will exceed the computational capabilities of the human race. "

Perhaps some of those projections are a little overwhelming. Maybe even a little frightening to you. But considering the changes you have personally witnessed and experienced in the past decade, this information probably doesn't seem so outlandish, either. We are living in an era when a single advancement in technology today can dramatically change the future of your business processes and operations. And in today's business climate, you cannot be wary of change; you cannot be semiconscious regarding semiconductors; you cannot be ignorant when it comes to imaging; and you must not become obstinate toward office automation.

The reality is that change is like a train. As a business owner or entrepreneur, you have three options regarding this high-tech train:
1. Stand on the platform and let it pass you by.
2. Get on the train and ride it to your destination.
3. Stand on the track and attempt to stop the train.

Let me assure you that no one has ever made a living—in this era or any other—by standing on the tracks and stopping trains. I'm not suggesting that you need to become a computer geek or a techno gadget guru to start a business. Nor am I promoting the idea of becoming your office's network know-it-all. You can easily become a technology addict, pouring unnecessary funds into gadgets, trinkets and devices that are simply not essential to turning a profit. For example, I do not need to equip my staff with cell phones that double as an MP3 player, a high-definition television screen, a photo album, a PlayStation, a heart monitor and an electronic GPS caddie for their golf games. But supplying them with phones that can access the Internet and their e-mail can be extremely advantageous to my business operations. When I took a vacation to Bermuda, I was able to answer 70 percent of my e-mail, via a Blackberry, while sitting on a beach with my wife. It was a huge tool for me, allowing me to get away without being completely out of touch. My employees also know that I am going to check that e-mail, via my phone, at some point every day when I am out of the office on business trips. In the past, I may have turned that phone off for meetings and not been able to get back with an employee who was attempting to serve a client or customer. So, the added expense of a PDA—as opposed to a regular phone—has added to my profits.

And these are the questions you must continually ask yourself and your employees regarding technology and other business operations: Will this make us more profitable? Will it make us more productive? Will it make us more service-friendly? Will it help us retain and recruit employees and customers?

Before I expound on how asking those questions has expanded my organization, let me be clear about exactly what I constitute as "Business Processes and Operations." Quite simply, they are the tools and processes of your respective trade that must be actively managed to make your business succeed. As I have pointed out previously, you don't need to spend a fortune to open a business. In my line of work, for example, to sell insurance you need a computer, access to the Internet, telephone and some well thought out sales and retention practices. That's it. Those are the vital components to opening an office. Those things make your office go. But you will need more to make it truly grow.

To be efficient, you must put some processes in place. At the time of this writing, we have more than 40,000 units in force in our agency. We have seven customer service representatives handling 40,000 lines of business from 15,000 customers. That would not be possible if I was utilizing the same, antiquated phone technology that I used when opening my first office. But with the advent of VoIP (voice over Internet protocol) it is now perfectly feasible and cost effective for my operation to run a call center of my own and to have one system manage main and branch offices and even remote and telecommuting workers. In a nutshell, VoIP is a method of taking analog audio signals, like the kind you hear when you talk on

the phone, and turning them into digital data that can be transmitted over the Internet. VoIP can turn a standard Internet connection into a way to place free phone calls. According to an article written by Jeff Noble on the site Practical Ecommerce, the technology for VoIP has been around since the 1970s, but it wasn't practical until recently because it requires a high-speed Internet connection or broadband. Quite frankly, I'm not exactly sure how it works. Nor do I care. What I know is that VoIP has made our organization more efficient. We can handle more calls than ever before, and we have more options than ever before such as call-waiting, call-forwarding, station assignment, remote operation, find-me/follow-me features, click-to-dial contacts with Microsoft Outlook integration and voicemail-as-email. It gives me the ability to talk from my office to another office without any costs. I have the hardware costs, but no cost for the phone line. I cut the middleman (AT&T) out of the plan.

I am already paying for an Internet connection, so why not plug my phone into the same connection and talk across the Internet to the other offices? The VoIP technology also allows me to go to Las Vegas, New York or virtually anywhere else, plug the IP phone into the wall and talk across the Internet for free. The technology also enables my employees to work from home at a very cost-effective rate. If, for example, I have a woman who wants to extend her maternity leave, but also wants to put in some hours, she can work from home, answering calls that are directed toward the main office. No one knows that she was answering calls while her newborn baby was sleeping, just as none of my clients realize I was answering e-mails while my wife was putting sunscreen on my back in Bermuda.

I am not going to get too specific on too many different technologies that have aided our operations. After all, VoIP may be old news by the time you are actually reading this. And one of the 3,000 books that are being published today may be on the latest telephone technology. But my point is this: You must continually ask yourself: Why are we doing things this way? Is there a better way? And what way is best for my business operations?

I use this personal example all the time, and—at the risk of sleeping on the couch when my wife reads this—I will share it with you. Shortly after we were married, Lisa cooked a ham for us and in preparing the ham, she cut both ends off it. My curiosity was instantly piqued. I asked her why she did it, and she said that is how her mom cooked hams. I nodded and let it pass, but I thought it was strange because I had never seen a ham cooked that way. Flash forward six months, and we are at Lisa's parents' house for Christmas. I walk into the kitchen and, sure enough, my mother-in-law, Brenda, is cutting off both ends of the ham. I ask her about it, and she tells me that is the way her mother did it. About a year later, we are at Lisa's grandmother's house, and she cooks a ham for Easter and starts by slicing off both ends of the ham. I asked her why she cooked her ham that way and she said, "Because my pan isn't big enough for the ham."

Three generations of women have spent most of their lives cutting off the ends of ham because Lisa's grandmother didn't have a pan that was big enough to hold it. How much ham has been wasted through the years? Probably enough to feed starving children in Ethiopia. Or at least enough to make some serious sandwiches. But no one ever asked, "Why are we doing it this way?"

Now that I have told you that story I am going to admit that I made the whole thing up. But it's a good example of what we do in our office settings—and in our personal lives—all the time. People in our country walk around with blinders on, doing the same things day after day, month after month and year after year simply because that's the way it has always been done. Why do you root for the Cowboys or the Astros or the Lakers or the Red Wings? Most people would say, "Because my dad did." Why do you mow your yard in a certain pattern? Is it because your dad taught you that way? Why do you set the table in a certain fashion? Why do you budget your expenses or balance your savings in a certain way? Why do you pay for all your restaurant tabs with cash?

There are some sacred cows that some people simply prefer to protect. If your grandfather rooted for the Bears because he was born in Chicago, that's fine. You may want to keep that as a family tradition that you pass down to your own children. But if your grandfather paid for everything in cash because he lived through the Great Depression, I challenge you to ask yourself, "Is that truly the best way for me?" Probably not, considering the advantages of paying by credit in today's society. Hear me out: I am not suggesting to live beyond your means or to purposely incur debt. What I am saying is that if you have enough in your budget for a $20 meal—and you also have a rewards program through your American Express or VISA account—wouldn't it be wise to pay through credit, accumulate rewards points and then pay off the balance when your statement is received? The answer is, "yes." You can pay for your personal or business travel expenses just by paying your day-to-day expenses with your VISA card. It takes a little discipline to pay off your balance at the end of the month, but if you develop that discipline, paying by credit can be so much more profitable to you. You are not belittling your grandfather's ways or spitting on family tradition; you are simply taking advantage of a market opportunity that didn't exist when your grandfather established a policy of paying only by cash.

From a business perspective, you could also be costing yourself untold amounts of income and employee productivity time by simply operating the way your grandfather, your father or your previous employer worked. Let me give you several examples of how we have increased productivity, saved money and generated more income by simply thinking "outside the box" and asking ourselves, "Why are we doing it this way?"

• TOGGLING: Here's a word that certainly didn't exist in Shakespeare's time, and it's one that is still—at least at the time of this writing—relatively unfamiliar in many business circles. Toggling is simply switching back and forth from one open document—or a website, e-mail account or spreadsheet—to another. If you work in front of a computer screen, there's a pretty good chance you have toggled by clicking your mouse to another document or hitting the "alt" and "tab" keys on your computer's keyboard. It's common practice in virtually every office in America. If you're a writer, you may be working on an article in Microsoft Word and researching information on various websites. You toggle back and forth, researching information on the Internet and using it to write your story. Or perhaps you have customer service agents working in your office, who are talking to a client on the phone while toggling back and forth from a policy to a spreadsheet to a website. Conventional wisdom suggests that this is just part of doing business in the 21st Century. But we asked ourselves, "Is this the best way to operate an office? Are we losing time, keeping clients on hold, as our reps toggle back and forth? Is there another way?" We decided to try placing two monitors on our customer service representatives' desks to reduce toggling. There was obviously an up-front cost to furnish a second monitor on these desks. But what we discovered is that by placing two monitors on the reps' desks, we were adding about 20 minutes of productivity to their day. That may not sound like much, but consider this: Twenty minutes a day for one employee amounts to 100 extra minutes per week. And over the course of a typical work year—50 weeks—that's an additional 5,000 minutes, or 83.3 hours. Now, let's say that I was paying that service rep $12 per hour. Over the course of one year, I added $999.60 worth of productivity to my office by spending $400 for a new monitor. Was it worth it? Absolutely. And that doesn't even take into account how many more customers we were able to serve in that additional 83.3 hours. With seven customer service reps, I added 583.1 hours of productivity in a year. It cost $2,800 for the monitors, but at $12 per hour, I added nearly $7,000 in production time. And in year two—once the monitors were in place—our productivity continued with no additional costs. I'd say it was worth it to look at our business processes and to study the habits of our employees.

• IMAGING: I am required, by state law, to keep all of my current and previous customers' insurance files for 10 years. As a result, I have an absolutely ridiculous amount of paper. I have three 10x10, air-conditioned warehouses full of document retention, which costs me $300 per month or $3,600 per year to rent that space. Every time I think about the volume of paper that I have stored in those warehouses it makes me sick to my stomach because my old method of operation was as archaic and unsophisticated as a cave man. Every policy was printed on paper, and finding a specific document in those warehouses is like trying to locate a needle in a haystack. Fortunately, technology has allowed me to discontinue the paper trail. With an imaging system, all of my incoming paperwork and back files can be stored not in warehouses, but on a computer hard drive. And if I need to look up a specific document, I can do it quickly and easily. We now store all of our files electronically and back them up on secure servers. But the imaging is truly amazing. Everything we receive in the mail from customers—photos, letters, even checks—is now imaged, so that we can retrieve it easily.

When I first started, I stored everything in filing cabinets. Then we went to an open-faced doctor office style filing system, with tabs on each end of the files. Before long, the filing system reached from the floor to the ceiling and covered about 30 feet of office wall space. From there, the dead files went to the storage warehouses, and this massive filing system required two full-time positions to maintain it. With imaging technology, we have been able to redirect staff members, save countless hours in locating files and become much more customer-friendly. Today, if a client calls our office to send a fax, the fax comes in as an image and the customer service person places it electronically into the appropriate client's file. No worries, no hassles, no wasted time and no paper.

With an image deposit scanner, we no longer have to make countless trips to the bank. We scan an image of the front and back of each check and, using state-of-the-art security features built into the image deposit scanner software, we make our daily deposits to our bank electronically. Not only is this a more safe and secure method, but it also can save you an amazing amount of man hours. Think about who you would send to the bank to deposit your checks each day. Would it be the lowest-paid newcomer on your staff? No, it would probably be one of the highest-paid employees, you or perhaps the CFO. How much time is lost daily, weekly and yearly if one of your top employees is battling traffic and sitting in line waiting for the next available drive-thru teller? Electronic check imaging can eliminate 80 to 90 percent of all your bank trips. There is an up-front cost to pay for the technology, but it's well worth every penny. Quite frankly, imaging is a technology advancement that is worth its weight in gold to me. And all it took was asking the question: "Is this paper trail the best way to operate?"

BEWARE OF TECHNOLOGY OVERLOAD

I will warn you in advance that plenty of technology salespeople are going to come into your office and say that they can do this and that for you. Most of their trinkets, gadgets, software, hardware and concepts are not going to be worth your time or money. But you, as the business owner, need to sit down and look at your business processes and ask: Why are we doing this? Is there a more effective way? Would this product or service help grow my business? If technology can make you more effective, and you can quickly recover the cost of the expense, it's probably a no-brainer.

Unlike my "cutting off the ends of the ham story," the following is absolutely true. When I was relatively new in the insurance business, I had left the office for an afternoon, and an employee called me in a panic because the computers had gone down. I asked what had been done about attempting to fix the problem, and my employee told me that she had called the help desk, and the technical service rep had informed her, based on the description she gave, that the computer was shot. A new hard drive would be required to fix the machine. At the end of the day, I came back to the office and discovered that we had lost an entire day of production. Nothing had happened. Knowing very little about computers, I went into the back, turned off the computer and unplugged it from the wall. When I turned it back on, the system came alive. So, I called the help desk and told them not to send a new hard drive because I had fixed it. Naturally, they asked me how I fixed it and I told them I unplugged it from the wall, plugged it back in and turned it back on. I was informed that this was known as a hard reboot. The woman on the other end of the phone line told me I should have never done this. "Why," I asked. She replied by saying that on page 13 of her manual it says you are never, ever to turn the computer off. I asked her if she ever thought through the reason it said that in the manual, and she responded by saying, "No, it just says not to do so in the manual." I told her it's probably because the machine communicates at night with the servers, and that's why you aren't supposed to turn it off. But if you weren't allowed to turn it off—under any circumstances—how would you ever turn it back on when the electricity went down. She had no answer for that because she had never thought outside the manual's box.

The fundamental point of including this story, however, is not to ridicule the service rep's narrow-minded, by-the-book approach. On the contrary, I think the important lesson to be learned here is that when attempting to solve a problem—especially in business—it is sometimes best to unplug the technology. Your machines, your software, your servers, your cell phones, etc. are important tools of the trade. But there are times when it is simply best to become unplugged.

Think about the term, "the good old days." If all this technology is so grand, why do so many people refer to the simpler, slower-paced times as, "the good old days?" I've got 500+ channels on my flat-screen HDTV, along with a DVR to record or rewind anything I might have missed. But honestly, there's very little worth watching on TV these days. In the words of the country and western band Rascal Flatts, " I miss Mayberry, sittin' on the porch ... watching the clouds roll by ... bye-bye" That song accurately summarizes what is so often missing in this fast-paced, technology-driven world that we live in today. In our personal and our professional lives, we are often missing the human touch. We send e-mails to fellow employees 15 feet away from our desks instead of walking over to them and asking a question face-to-face. We send text-messages to clients instead of giving them a personal call. We teleconference instead of meeting with people. We visit websites instead of neighbors. We even try to find our soul mates in cyberspace. (One

PERSONALIZE

out of every eight couples who married in 2006 met online). It's becoming a very impersonal world in which we live.

Am I suggesting that we give up all of our gadgets? Trash all of our technological trinkets? Sabotage our semiconductors? Attempt to build a future by using yesteryear's strategies and technologies?

No, no, no and no way. I just made a point of saying that grandpa's strategies—or even dad's—are not necessarily the best way to conduct business just because it worked for him. You always need to look for ways to utilize new tools and technologies. Keep yourself updated and abreast of the latest advances; read industry-specific technology publications; be willing to sit down with some technology salespeople; and be willing to attend some technology conferences. Some of the seminars that I regularly attend have nothing to do with selling insurance. In the last 15 years, for example, I have gone to hear technology expert Steve Anderson speak about implementing technology into business. I have never left one of those seminars without some fresh ideas and perspectives.

With all of that said, however, remember that your business still boils down to relationships. And you do not build too many long-lasting relationships by e-mailing, text-messaging, instant-messaging, etc. Those tools can help you maintain a relationship, but they are not going to help you build a new one. And they are certainly not the key to closing a business deal.

Let's look at e-mail momentarily. It is obviously an amazing tool that has revolutionized the way we work and we communicate. But in my personal opinion, it is also overused and obtrusive. Whenever a new person—most often a younger person— comes to work for us, I usually have to coach him or her about not relying solely on e-mail. No matter how convenient e-mail is, we are still a verbal society. If Joe is my new

120

employee, he may e-mail or instant-message me inside our own office several times a day with questions about his responsibilities or how to perform specific duties. But it's been my experience that e-mails are not usually very thorough. One answer on an e-mail generally leads to another question. The electronic dialogue continues back and forth throughout the day. On the other hand, if Joe would have gotten his butt out of his chair and come to see me, his questions would have undoubtedly been answered much more thoroughly.

In dealing with clients, it is almost always better to pick up the phone rather than sending out an e-mail. If a client needs a document quickly, I can easily attach it to an e-mail and send it to him. He has the document instantly instead of in a couple of days. That's using technology to benefit your business. But if a client e-mails me with a complaint, I will pick up the phone to answer him or her. One of the huge problems with e-mail, instant-messaging, text-messaging and other text-related communications technology is that the receiver of the message cannot determine the tone of my words. As such, my message can be easily misinterpreted.

For example, if a client e-mails me about a customer service agent in my office, complaining about a negative experience he or she had with my employee, I could reply to the e-mail with the following:

Dear Joe Client: I am very disappointed to learn about the negative experience you had in working with Suzy Service Agent. Customer satisfaction is our top priority here at The Barhorst Insurance Group, and I have talked to Suzy about your negative experience. She has long been my top customer service agent, so I am surprised by this negative experience. Fortunately, with our voice over Internet protocol telephone system, we record all of our calls. Together, Suzy and I will listen to the recording of the phone call that you and Suzy had so that we can determine where any misinterpretations may have been made. We sincerely appreciate your business, and we look forward to serving you in the future.

Joe Client may be satisfied with that reply or he may be livid. He doesn't know if I am communicating to him in a heartfelt tone or a smart-ass one. While the customer is always right, I don't want to hang Suzy out to dry without having listened to the call, either. So, I am careful not to say that Suzy was in the wrong. Depending on his mood and level of frustration, the word "misinterpretation" may also send Joe off the deep end. And he may take the sentence about Suzy being a top customer service agent in the wrong way. He may take it as me saying that he should not feel the way he feels or that everyone else has always been pleased with Suzy, so he must be the problem. He may fire off a reply to me saying that there was no misinterpretation and that Suzy acted like a spoiled brat, which would require me to reply back to him. In the end, it would have been so much easier to have picked up the phone and called Joe. He could detect my tone, I could answer his concerns, and at the end of the conversation, he would probably feel like he was important enough client for me to pick up the phone to call him.

There's just no substitute in a situation like that for picking up the phone. Nor is there a substitute for a hand-written letter when it comes to thanking a customer or potential client. I have received e-mail thank-you notes, and I discard them as quickly as the junk mail that manages to find its way through our filters. But a hand-written thank-you note—even if it's nothing more than two sentences and a signature—says to that customer or client that he or she made an impression on you. It would be easier and cheaper to send an e-mail, but that stamp and that hand-written note could deliver a long-term association.

None of this is rocket science, of course. It's common sense. But you, as a business owner, must monitor your own actions and the actions of your employees when it comes to the use of technology. I have found that one of the best business practices for my office is to turn off my e-mail account throughout much of the day. If you have pop-up messages alerting you of incoming e-mails, it will run your day. It's human nature to want to see what the message is about, how it applies to you, etc. If you are involved in a project that should take you two hours, it can easily take three hours or more if you are constantly being interrupted by pop-up messages. Even if you are only deleting them, those pop-ups interfere with your train of thought. And if you are actually opening those e-mails as they come into your account, answering them, following the links that they include, forwarding them to the proper location and so forth, your two-hour project can turn into an all-day affair. Turn off your e-mail during high-volume hours at work and set aside specific times to check your e-mail, and only check it at those times. That way you can get done what you need to get done. And one more word to the wise about e-mail: The worst thing you can do is to answer your e-mails first thing in the morning because it wastes so much of your time. If you have five things on your to-do list when you walk into the office in the morning, get those done first before answering your e-mails. Inevitably, opening that e-mail account will add five things to your task list.

In a couple of years—or even a couple of days—the technological advances I have discussed in this chapter will probably be as outdated as the VHS tape. Technology is changing our world and the way we do business faster than we could have ever imagined 10 years ago. As Daniel prophesized thousands of years ago, "many will go here and there to increase knowledge." I'm not sure if these are the end times that he was referring to, but in regards to technology in the workplace, you, as the business owner, need to keep end goals in mind. Stay abreast of what is happening in the world around you; take off the blinders; don't be afraid to ask yourself and your employees if there is another, better way of doing things; and constantly examine your business processes and always try to improve a little each day. In respect to Daniel, I'll do a little prophesizing of my own here: If you can keep your business on top of modern technology while maintaining old-fashioned values and core principles, you will be amazed at how quickly you can travel down that road to success. You've got what it takes, and if you are staying up with technology, you probably also have a GPS Navigation System to help you get there.

GAME DAY PREP

1. Predictions are that by the year 2049:
   A. The Chicago Cubs will be the most dominant franchise in MLB history.
   B. Peace will exist in the Middle East.
   C. A typical $1,000 computer will exceed the computational capabilities of the human race.
   D. Elvis will finally come out of hiding.
   Answer here _____

2. Regarding technology and other business operations, you need to continually ask yourself:
   A. Why are we doing things this way? Is there a better way? And what way is best for my personal business operations?
   B. Will this make us more profitable? Will it make us more productive? Will it make us more service-friendly? Will it help us retain and recruit customers?
   C. What's for lunch?
   D. Both A and B, but certainly not C.
   Answer here _____

3. Even in this high-tech age in which we live, when communicating with customers and clients on important matters, it is almost always best to:
   A. Pick up the phone and call them or schedule a face-to-face meeting.
   B. Send an e-mail to them and include them on your mass distribution list for all e-mail jokes.
   C. Text them on their cell phones using warm, fuzzy codes like TFYB (thanks for your business) and WYDBWU, YAPOOF (when you do business with us, you are part of our family).

D. Direct them to your website so you can stop wasting your time talking to individuals about their personal concerns.

Answer here_____

More detailed information about the topics covered in this chapter is available at www.gameplanbook.com. 👉

The website is continually updated to provide the latest information, forms, instructions and tips to help you build or grow your business.

Extra Points - Notes

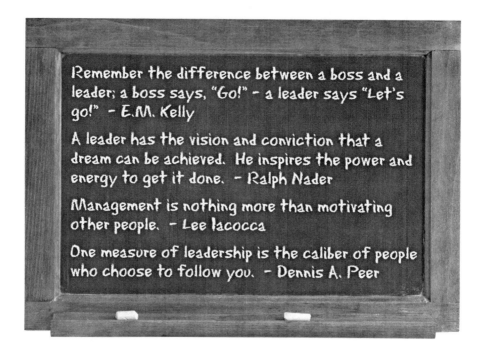

Remember the difference between a boss and a leader; a boss says, "Go!" – a leader says "Let's go!" – E.M. Kelly

A leader has the vision and conviction that a dream can be achieved. He inspires the power and energy to get it done. – Ralph Nader

Management is nothing more than motivating other people. – Lee Iacocca

One measure of leadership is the caliber of people who choose to follow you. – Dennis A. Peer

CHAPTER 6

HUMAN CAPITAL: THE POWER OF PEOPLE

Okay, folks, it's quiz time. Here we are in Chapter 6, and we have covered an abundance of technical information and provided plenty of real-life examples in the past few sections. We have broken down business plans and bank loans; we've covered co-ops and contacts; and we've addressed sales techniques. We've looked at technology and trends; we've discussed thinking outside the box, but inside the donut box; and we've cited examples from Biblical characters, professional research groups, business leaders. We've covered an awful lot of ground, and it is my hope that the business-specific material we have dissected and discussed in recent chapters has provided you with some detailed information that you can implement into your own business practices and plans. It is also my hope that you have been taking notes—and not naps—as you have read through the material.

Either way, it's about time for a short pop quiz. No need to sweat; no need to flip back through the previous pages; and no need to strain your brain. This should be pretty easy stuff. So, here goes:

Pop Quiz

Q: What is the first thing you need to do before opening your own business or expanding your current operations?

A: _____

Q: If you decide to act on only one principle in this entire book, what do I most vehemently and vigorously advise you to do?

A: _____

Q: What is the underlying message of virtually every self-help, motivational and entrepreneurial book that has ever been written? And what's the fundamental point of practically every success seminar that has ever been presented?

A: _____

I am going to assume that you nailed this quiz and that you are
now doing a pretty good impersonation of Triumph's Rik Emmett
or Aerosmith's Steven Tyler. As the administrator of this quiz, I
would accept either one of these two answers:

1. Hold Onto to Your Dreams

2. Dream On

Hopefully, you recall that I spent the entire first chapter talking
about—or perhaps preaching about—the importance of your own
dreams. I also hope that you have long since joined the "5 percent
group," an elite and focused segment of society that actually
writes down their dreams, goals and visions. And hopefully, you
are spending a considerable amount of time revisiting and revising
them. If not, there's a strong chance that your focus will start to
fade, and you will eventually
end up wondering where your
life's course went astray as you
spend your post-retirement years
gathering shopping carts in the
parking lot of Wal-Mart.

Sorry. Perhaps I got a little carried away
with the Wal-Mart comment. But by now
you should know how strongly I believe
in the power of dreaming and writing your
goals, hopes and aspirations down on paper.
I believe it increases your chances of success
by 95 percent, and I am convinced that it is an absolutely vital step
to achieving your heart's desires. Constantly visualize yourself
living in the house you want, driving the car you want, enjoying
the career success you want…and your subconscious mind will
eventually find a way to make it happen. That's my No. 1 secret of
success.

Now, I want to let you in on my No. 2 secret, which will allow you
to exceed your own wildest expectations: Teach your employees
to dream, encourage them to write down their goals and help them

to achieve their visions. If you put a serious emphasis on helping your employees achieve their dreams, you will likely be amazed at how far it takes you and your business. I cannot emphasize this enough. A business plan will keep you on the right track; acquiring business funding and marketing your company can enable you to hit the ground running; making your own contacts and making your own sales will pay the bills and keep the creditors away; technology can vastly improve your day-to-day operations. But if you truly want to grow your business and generate the lifestyle that you envision, you are ultimately going to need to invest in people. Your own people. You need to be able to duplicate your own efforts by hiring great employees…not just warm bodies. And the only way to get great people to buy into your visions for your business is to help them develop and achieve their own dreams. When I am looking for employees I am hoping to find people who are even more driven, more motivated and more intelligent than me. And ultimately, I'd like to see them be even more successful than me. Seriously. I don't even care if they eventually outgrow me and go off into a different career path or open up their own company. In fact, I'll even help them do that. They don't have to hide from me or go behind my back in making a career move up the ladder of success. I'll help them take the necessary steps; I'll hold the ladder for them as they climb, because if they are that motivated, that productive and that successful, my business will benefit as they grow.

The short-sighted, holier-than-thou mentality of some business owners, managers and executives never ceases to amaze me. Some otherwise sharp businesspeople often lose perspective when it comes to their own employees. They want to be viewed as kings of their domain, and they often view their employees as peasants, not partners. They want to pay their employees as little as they can, boss them around as much as they can and keep them in shackles as long as they can. Maybe it's an ego thing. Perhaps it's a power trip. Or possibly it's some deep-seeded insecurity issues. Whatever the case, it's an absolutely absurd way to run your business. Your employees are your most valuable asset, and they are the key to growing your business. The better people you find, the more profitable you will be. The better you help them look, the better you will look. If you take the emphasis off yourself and help your employees fulfill their dreams, your own dreams will come true on a much grander scale than you could have ever imagined.

As I stated earlier in this book, my initial goal as a business owner was simply to get to a point where my wife and I were grossing $20,000 a month. That was my dream; my vision; my mission; my motivation; and—at the time—my ultimate goal. Nowadays, I look back at the number and laugh. We have greatly exceeded that number, and the primary reason for that is because we have hired great people. Let me re-emphasize that point: **IT'S NOT ALL ABOUT ME.** And as a business owner, **IT'S NOT ALL ABOUT YOU**. You can try to go it alone, and you can work yourself into the ground and achieve some level of success. Starting off, you may have to do just that. In fact, it was all about me in the beginning. But no longer. At some point in time, you must expand your staff to grow your business, as your own efforts can only take you so far. And often the difference between a successful business and a bankrupt one can be traced to the quality of the employees.

Floundering and failing businesses are too often the by-product of poor hiring and firing practices, and far too many business owners have gone bankrupt because they failed to understand the importance of surrounding themselves with great people. No matter what industry you are involved with and no matter how far along you are in your business, you must understand that your **personal** success or failure may ultimately be determined by your **personnel** success or failure.

Now, let me be completely honest in saying that we've hired a few duds and some dopes during my career as a business owner that have tested my patience and negatively affected my bottom line. But we've learned from those mistakes and have developed a personnel system that has become a critical component of our business operations. As a result of that system, we've hired many visionaries, and we've helped them to develop their own dreams. We've hired goal-oriented go-getters, and we have simply provided them with the tools, training and techniques to succeed. We've built a talented team, and that team has taken us to heights that we could have never envisioned 15-to-20 years ago. I started out with the vision of becoming the most dynamic and successful insurance salesman in Houston. But as I write today I can honestly say that I am not even the best insurance salesman in my own agency. Does that bother me? Does that hurt my ego? Does that cause me to question my self-worth?

No. No way. And hell no. Who cares about self worth? My net worth has

EMPOWER doubled, tripled, quadrupled, etc. because I was able to recruit and hire some great salespeople. I have mentored them; I have provided the capital to get them started; I have trained them and encouraged them; I have taught them to set their goals and write down their dreams; and I have helped them achieve their own visions of success. My monetary reward has been handsome, as I have earned a percentage of their profits. If I can help make multiple millionaires, I become a multi-millionaire. I simply sold them on the fact that my business could help them achieve their visions.

While there are thousands—and perhaps even hundreds of thousands—of great examples of business leaders selling their employees on the power of their dreams, one of my all-time favorites involves the controversial and passionate owner of the Dallas Mavericks, Mark Cuban. By 1995, when Cuban and his business partner, Todd Wagner, started a business called Audio Net in Dallas, Cuban was already an accomplished businessman. As far back as when he was 12, he had started his own business, selling garbage bags door-to-door in his Pittsburgh neighborhood. He also had four or five other business ventures while in high school, and he put himself through college at Indiana by giving disco lessons to sorority houses and operating a chain letter. He then moved to Texas and was fired from his first job as a computer salesman. Although he was the No. 1 salesman in the company, he was fired because he refused to vacuum after work. But he used the knowledge he gained from that job to start Micro Solutions, a computer-consulting firm he sold several years later to CompuServe for $6 million. "I ended up making about $2.2 million," Cuban told CBS correspondent Steve Kroft on 60 Minutes. "I bought a lifetime pass on American Airlines and I just started traveling. If you would have asked me what my occupation was the day after that, it was retired. I turned 31 the day after we sold it."

He obviously didn't stay retired for too long. Like him or loathe him, Cuban is a visionary; he is powered by an entrepreneurial spirit. And when his old college buddy, Wagner, presented him with a business opportunity in 1995, Cuban came out of retirement. In essence, the vision for Audio Net was inspired by Wagner's and Cuban's desire to listen to Indiana basketball games in Dallas. They bought a $3,000 computer and went to work on transmitting radio broadcasts across the Internet. They hired a few people and sold them on the possibilities of the business. "We couldn't have had more than 20 employees," Cuban said on the FOX Sports program *Beyond the Glory*. "I said, 'Look, I have no idea where this is going to go, but one thing I will guarantee you: In five years, this thing is either going to be worth billions of dollars and we're all going to be millionaires…or we're going to be out of business and we'll just be friends. There's going to be no in-between."

With Cuban pushing his salespeople to the limit, Audio Net began to grow. They soon put up the first radio station and TV station on the Internet. From there, it went to 380 radio stations and 40 TV stations. It also broadcast 16,000 live events, including a Victoria's Secret fashion show and President Clinton's Grand Jury testimony. By 1998, the company had more than 300 employees and a new name: Broadcast.com. They then went public, going on a road show to attract investors. Original stock in Broadcast.com was offered at $18 a share when it opened on the stock market on the morning of July 17, 1998. The closing price that day had leapt to $62.75, an increase of 248 percent. At that time it was the biggest initial public offering in the history of the stock market.

You may have heard that part of the story before. But here's the part that really impresses me the most about Cuban: He and Wagner directed the Broadcast.com choir, but Cuban made sure that he had good people around him to make the company sing. And he also understood how to utilize his employees' specific talents. He was smart enough to move people around so that a baritone wasn't trying to play the role of a soprano. After the company went public, friends and family who had shown enough faith to make the initial investment of $16,000 were worth nearly $20 million apiece. And 300 of the company's 334

UTILIZE SKILLS

Leaders don't create followers, they create more leaders. - Tom Peters

employees were instant millionaires. One of those employees had a pretty unique story. "My second employee was a girl by the name of April, and she almost got fired the first day," Cuban said on *Beyond the Glory.* "Todd asked her to make copies, and she did them backward. She was faxing things upside down all day. But we moved her out of being an (administrative assistant) and moved into another area where she could do things well. The difference between being fired and moving her into another area where she could do well was worth about $20-something million to her."

A year after the public offering, Cuban and Wagner sold Broadcast. com to Yahoo for stock options worth more than $6 billion. Cuban's first purchase—obtained online—was a private jet, a Gulfstream V, for $41 million. His next purchase was the Dallas Mavericks for $280 million. And you probably know the rest of the story. Today, Cuban is one of the wealthiest and most recognizable businessmen in America.

There are a number of reasons for his success. But chief among them may be his ability to inspire his employees and to sell them on achieving their own dreams. While he has often displayed a Midas touch in his business deals, remember that Cuban didn't become a billionaire on his own efforts and merits. He became a billionaire by helping his employees become millionaires. That's an important distinction to remember as a business owner.

NEVER STOP RECRUITING

My goal in hiring people is always this: Find a allstar. I realize I'm certainly not alone in that regard. Practically every business owner or manager sets out with a goal of hiring great people. But I believe I may differ from the vast majority of CEO-types in several areas.

First of all, I am always, always, always on the lookout for that next allstar. You can't always recruit great people to your organization by simply placing an advertisement in the newspaper or website. And you won't always find the next allstar when you have an opening. You must be on the lookout for that unique, service-oriented person wherever you go, 365 days per year.

If you're talking to somebody at the counter of McDonald's, and you like the way he or she presents service to you, recruit them. Get their name; get a phone number and file that number where you can find it. You may find your star service rep of the future when ordering a Big Mac®. And your sales star of tomorrow may be helping you find a blouse for your wife or a tie for your husband at Dillard's. Open your eyes and your ears when you are shopping, dropping off your cleaning, working out at the gym, taking your family out to eat, etc.

I am constantly on the lookout for energetic, engaging people who have the right stuff. And when I find those people, I make it a point to tell them that I am a business owner and that I am impressed by their service skills. I make sure to acquire contact information from that person and I then build a database of contacts I can call when I decide the time is right to add a new person, create a new position or fill an existing vacancy on my staff. I would also teach all of your employees the same process. The more company advocates you have the more qualified candidates you will find.

I do this because I never want to "settle" for the best of the least. Many business owners believe that all you need to do to hire someone is to place an ad in the newspaper or on an Internet site like Monster.com. You may get

HIRE = ATTITUDE

> The best executive is the one who has sense
> enough to pick good men to do what he wants
> done, and self-restraint enough to keep from
> meddling with them while they do it.
> – Theodore Roosevelt

lucky and find a diamond in the rough by this method, but it's definitely not a sure thing. Most often, the movers and shakers that you most want to hire are not browsing the want ads every day. So, what you frequently receive is a bunch of resumes from disgruntled workers who are hoping the grass is greener in your business. If you are looking for "grass grazers," rely only on the want ads.

Now, let me say that you can occasionally find great employees with a want ad. Sometimes a potentially standout employee is stuck in a dead end role or being shackled by a deadbeat boss. If that's the case, a go-getter could be surfing Monster.com. So, I am certainly not discouraging you from placing that ad. But I strongly encourage you to supplement the resumes you receive from the ad with your own list that you have been compiling for weeks, months or years. Hiring a headhunter or a search firm can be costly and is often a waste of time. Just open your eyes and ears and be aware of the people around you. If you pay a little attention, you just may find that the best receptionist for your business is currently behind the counter at the fast food chain where you take your kids on Saturdays. And the sales star of the future could be the young man at Home Depot—the guy who actually helped you go home with the right part for the repair this time. If you are constantly hunting for great people, you will know where to turn when the time is right to hire someone.

THE HIRING PROCESS

Admission time: Fairly recently, I fired a woman who had been with us for 18 months. She was miserable in our office environment; we were not pleased with her, either. It was a match made in Hades, not Heaven. I tell you this because I want you to know that my hiring process is not 100 percent bulletproof. I've spent nearly 15 years developing, testing and fine-tuning the process, and it's pretty darned good. But it's not foolproof. No process is infallible, which is important to understand. People can fool you during the interview process. They can dress themselves up; they can project professionalism; they can engage you with sparkling personality traits; they can dazzle you with  what you perceive to be brilliance. Then they show up to work, and you discover that you have actually hired a slouch in a suit. French author Jules Renard once wrote that, "Laziness is nothing more than the habit of resting before you get tired." I've mistakenly hired a few of those folks, which can be extremely costly in terms of your productivity, your time, your aspirin supply for the amount of headaches endured and your bottom-line profits. So, developing a detailed hiring process is extremely important to your business. It won't totally eliminate mistakes, but it can dramatically improve your hiring success ratio. A word of advice: Make sure that your legal representation evaluates your hiring process so that it complies with state and federal employment guidelines.

I won't walk you through our detailed hiring process (go to www. gameplanbook.com for the entire process). But I want to make one thing abundantly clear about the candidates you bring in for an interview: DON'T ASSUME. In the previous section, I encouraged you to always be on the lookout for potential hires. But no matter how well that person looked to you in another environment, don't assume that he or she will automatically fit in your office. The same goes with your friends, colleagues, associates, family members, etc. DO NOT ASSUME ANYTHING ABOUT THEM.

DON'T ASSUME

Just because your next-door neighbor displays a meticulous attention to detail in landscaping, maintaining his automobile, keeping his garage clean, disciplining his children and so forth, do not assume that he would show that same attention to detail in your office or establishment. And just because your cousin has an impressive track record in selling widgets, do not assume that he will be just as productive in selling your products. Put your closest associates, your prime contacts and your best friends through the same hiring process that you administer to the strangers who answered your ad. Do not blow off the hiring processes because of your personal relationship with any candidate. Many, many well-meaning business owners and managers have been haunted by "my best friend's sister" or "my neighbor's cousin" because, while they may look good in a social setting, they may absolutely suck at work. Establish a hiring process, and put everyone—and I mean EVERYONE—through it.

Okay, let me climb off the soap box and walk you through a high-level glance at our hiring process. Before we ever even consider bringing candidates into our office, we conduct a resume screening on them—as well as a telephone screening. We examine the resumes we receive to make certain that their education is relevant. And by "relevant," I mean this: Is their education or training something that correlates with our business? Then we go through a checklist of questions: Is their work experience relevant? What have they been doing with their time? Are there gaps in their resume? You just go through the resumes with other members of your current staff—or your spouse or advisor if you do not yet have a staff—and call out those things. If a candidate has had five jobs in the past five years, why hire her? She's just going to stay with you for eight or nine months and then go. I'm also looking for some particular things on a resume, such as some community service. I want to know if a person is committed to his community, because that means there is less of a chance of him jumping at the next opportunity that comes along. And if he's not necessarily committed to his community, I want to see that he is committed to a cause. I'm also looking for advancement in the last job. I want to see if the candidate has been promoted; I want to see his or her achievements and accomplishments.

Once I've thoroughly examined the resumes and weeded out the ones that would simply be a waste of my time, I take the next step—or have someone on my staff do it—and place a phone call to the candidate. I want to hear how the candidate speaks; I want to hear if there is enthusiasm in her voice; and I want to hear how she responds to my questions. Remember this: You're looking for stars, not wimps. Your business success could depend on this person's ability to handle scrutiny or objections. You don't want fragile, frail, feeble weaklings; you want a confident, capable conqueror. So, you should not lob only softball questions during this conversation. Ask some tough questions.

When someone impresses me during the phone interview, the next step in our hiring process is to bring him/her into the office and to give the candidate a basic personality profile. This may seem like a waste of time to some of you, as it once did to me. But trust me on this: You can save yourself so many headaches and place your people in the right position for success by administering a simple personality test. This goes for your current employees, as well. I am a major proponent of personality evaluations, as these tests can help you understand why your employees react to situations differently, and they can help you tailor your motivational techniques, your training seminars and your overall planning. They can also help you create a more harmonious office setting because everyone understands each other's personality type. This is not some newfangled concept, either. According to the website

PERSONALITY

MATCH SKILLS

uniquelyyou.net, the first model of human behavior was introduced by Hippocrates some 400 years before Christ as the "Four Temperament Types." It identified four classic types: Choleric, Sanguine, Phlegmatic and Melancholy to describe human behavior and personality insights. In 1929, William Marston changed the old Greek titles to: Dominant, Inspirational, Submissive, and Compliant—which have become known as the "DISC Personality Types." Through extensive research, Carl Jung, Katharine C. Briggs and Isabel Briggs Myers later identified sixteen personality types.

Nowadays, you can find various personality tests on the Internet that can suit your needs from an evaluation standpoint. These can be especially valuable in terms of your own growth and self-development, as well as building a cohesive business team. Simply do an Internet search for "personality tests" and do a little research. Before you purchase one, make sure it is applicable to your business and provides you the answers that you're seeking. The test I chose places people into four categories: enterprisers, motivators, analyzers and togetherness. When I first got the test I wanted to make sure I had my current employees seated at the right place on the bus. I had each employee take the survey to determine their personality type. We then held a session with all the employees sharing techniques on how to work with different personality types.

Do not try to fit a square peg in a round hole when it comes to placing employees. It won't work for them; it won't work for you. People will tell you they are this or that in the interview process. Many of them want the job so desperately that they will pretend to be something that they are not. But in the long run, you cannot expect an analyzer to effectively fill the role of a motivator. If you are seeking an enterpriser, don't hire a togetherness person. Administer the personality profile, and you will be much happier and the employee will be a much better fit.

Many people probably recall the well-publicized case of college football coach George O'Leary in 2001. O'Leary was hired as the head coach of Notre Dame in December of 2001. Five days later, he resigned after admitting that he had lied about his academic and athletic background. O'Leary claimed to have a master's degree in education and to have played college football for three years, but checks into his background showed those statements not to be true. A biography released by Notre Dame when it announced his hiring said O'Leary received a master's degree from New York University in 1972. Upon closer inspection, however, it was discovered that, while O'Leary was a student there, he did not receive a degree.

Furthermore, he never earned a letter playing football at New Hampshire, although his biography claimed he earned three. New Hampshire officials said he never played in a game. The whole ordeal was a huge black eye—and not just for O'Leary. Notre Dame looked pretty foolish, as well. And unfortunately, lying on a resume is common practice. At my son's high school there was a coach that didn't have a degree. He lied about the whole thing, saying that he was a Texas A&M graduate. He never graduated. So, be careful; and do not take everything on a resume as 100 percent factual. Perform a background check. It could prevent you from hiring a fibber or— much worse than that—a felon.

After the personality profile has been administered, we give our candidates EIQ and IQ tests. We use the well-known IQ test to identify candidates with average or better intelligence. However, significant research suggests that a person's emotional intelligence (EIQ) might be a greater predictor of success than his or her intellectual intelligence (IQ), despite an assumption that people with high IQs will naturally accomplish more in life. That's not necessarily the case.

The next step involves giving our candidates a values survey. It's simply a list of 100 words on a sheet of paper and they rank the 10 most important. It's something that you can do yourself. You might list workplace things such as: professional atmosphere, retirement plan, health benefits, flexibility in schedule, no overtime, leadership

VALUES opportunities, positive relationship with co-workers, technology, training opportunities and salary.

I just interviewed a guy and number ten on his list was money, and number one was leadership. Some of the answers they provide may be total B.S., as they may be answering how they think I want them to answer. But the nice thing about the values survey is that two years from now, when I'm reviewing or meeting with this guy and he's complaining to me about money I'm going to say, "That was number 10 on your list. You told me you wanted to spend the most time working on leadership in the company. You didn't say you wanted more money, you said you wanted us to invest in you as a leader."

I realize that most business owners and managers do not administer this many tests or require their job applicants to jump through so many hoops. But that's also why most businesses tend to settle for warm bodies instead of finding the person best suited for the job. I am looking for detail-oriented, determined people who are willing to go the extra mile. So, right off the bat, I want to see if the applicant is willing to go beyond what she may typically expect in terms of qualifying for the job.

Only after all the tests have been administered and forms have been signed do I actually sit down with a candidate for an interview. And there is a specific step-by-step method that should be followed in the interview process, as well. Many companies will immediately tell the candidate about the position, how great the company is, etc. DON'T! You're not trying to sell the candidate on the job yet; you're trying to qualify him. So, the first words to come out of your mouth need to be this: "Tell me about yourself. Tell me what you like to do with your free time. Tell me about your high school and college experiences. Tell me about your hobbies." Don't worry about job specifics right away. He wouldn't be in your office after all the preliminary screening you have done if he didn't have skill that interested you. What you're looking to find out now is how this person would fit in your company environment. And no matter what he says, do not react in astonishment, amazement, shock, horror or anything other than matter-of-fact. If a guy volunteers that he left his last job because he had an affair with his secretary, don't react negatively. If you do—and he's a smart person—he's going to realize he's going the wrong direction in the interview and needs to change his pitch. You want him to open up; you want to see how he reacts to a person that doesn't give him a strong feel—one way or the other. This needs to be all about him and what makes him tick. You want to know if he is an avid golfer—and what exactly that means. Does he enjoy playing with buddies on the weekend? Or is he so obsessed with the game that he will skip out early every day to work on it in hopes of earning his PGA card? You also want to know about his home life. If there are problems at home, it will eventually be brought to work. If everything else was equal, I would choose the candidate with more stability at home almost every time. Again, you will save yourself plenty of headaches, lost production time and a world of drama by choosing stability.

At some point during the interview, the candidate is going to ask you specifics about the job and the company. It's not the time to discuss those issues. Politely say something like: "It's our policy not to discuss job specifics during the first interview. During the second interview, we will address each and every one of your questions to your full satisfaction." Before the candidate leaves this first interview, we request that he writes a letter detailing why he is the right person for the job. You would be amazed by how many candidates eliminate themselves from consideration during this step—by either not writing a letter or writing an extremely poor one.

The next step is to bring the top two or three candidates back for another interview and to eliminate all the others. Any time the process kicks someone out, we always send them a rejection letter that says, "Thanks for inquiring about a position with the Barhorst Insurance Group. We appreciate your time, but other candidates have better matched what we're looking for in this particular position."

During the second interview is when you start selling the position and your company. Talk about your visions, your previous accomplishments, your stability, your benefits package and anything else that is a positive selling point for your business. By now,

the candidate should be comfortable with you, and this is the best time to handle all of his questions about the job. Be completely honest here. Do not promise a corner office with a view when you have a cubicle in mind for the candidate. If you promise the moon, you had better be prepared to deliver it when he takes the job. You want to sell him on your business, but you do not want to oversell.

At the end of this second interview, we administer one more profile—the Benchmark Profile. This profile takes the top-performing people in your office—your existing employees—and compares their answers to the candidate's answers. One of my top salespeople is named Mark Farris, and I have his answers on file. So, when Paul Prospect takes the Benchmark Profile, I can compare the answers and see that Paul is similar to Mark in this regard and different in that one.

Now you have the results of four profiles and two personal interviews to help you base your decision in making the right hire. Many times that is enough data and information to make a decision, but if there are still two highly qualified candidates left, I will bring them in for a third interview and also bring in a third party interviewer to help me conduct the final stage. If I did the first two interviews, I may have connected with one of the candidate more than the other, and I may have interviewer bias. So, I'm going to step out of the room and have someone else interview the candidates and make sure we're seeing similar traits and qualities.

The entire process may seem detail oriented, but it's not difficult. It's taken me roughly 15 years to build and now it works extremely well. Our hiring success ratio is off the charts compared to many of our competitors, which is evident by the amount of industry awards we're receiving. If you want a good business, you better surround yourself with good people. And if you want a great business, find great people. You don't find those people by simply placing an ad and relying on your "gut feel" after one interview. You may not choose to follow my entire hiring process, but I'd advise you to follow it rather closely. I was recently on a consulting call, and I showed a gentleman with a $200 million business our hiring strategy. I have a $50 million operation and he says, "I need this right now." Our strategy isn't perfect, but it works. Statistics show that there is about a 30 percent success rate in hiring insurance agents across the country, while our success rate is 70 percent. The key to that success is following the process we've built.

If people disclose their background problems up front, then we won't hold it against them. So, if Paul Prospect put on the background form that he received a DWI in 1997, that may actually be a positive on his behalf—depending on how he explains the situation to me. First, it shows that he is honest. I would certainly discuss that with him during the process, but I know that anyone is entitled to making a mistake. If he did not disclose that information up front, however, I would immediately eliminate him from consideration when it was revealed on the background check.

You are looking for people with integrity. So, don't make exceptions when you're hiring. Whenever a flag pops up with a candidate and its telling you, "no," listen to the flag. Don't go against the flag if it's saying "no."

Establish a process, have your legal representation examine it thoroughly and follow it. And when you are tempted to take shortcuts in the hiring process or do a favor for a buddy, remember this: Your **personal** success or failure may ultimately be determined by your **personnel** success or failure.

> You do not lead by hitting people over the head. That's assault, not leadership.
> - Dwight D. Eisenhower

RETAINING, TRAINING, ALIGNING AND MOTIVATING

I loved the way Mike Ditka coached; I admired the way Paul "Bear" Bryant drove his players beyond the breaking point; I think Bobby Knight's record speaks for itself, making him one of the greatest basketball coaches in the history of the sport; and it's hard to argue with the track record of former New York Yankees manager Billy Martin. They were all great leaders in their respective sports and in their time. But if you try to lead your company—in this day and age—with Ditka's volatility, Bryant's tenacity, Knight's explosiveness or Martin's rage, you're office is eventually going to be awfully lonely and your bank account will become a blank account.

Occasionally being stern is necessary; laying down the law is sometimes effective; demanding excellence is a positive attribute. But ruling your business with an iron fist is a flawed management style that will leave you in a world of hurt. I started off this chapter by giving you the key to exceeding your wildest dreams: Teach your employees to dream, encourage them to write down their goals and help them to achieve their visions.

You can't create a nightmare environment and then encourage people to chase their dreams. You can't build positive team chemistry by constantly breaking people down. You can't keep your staff on the same page when you are constantly ripping them a new one. And you can't create a warm environment for your clients when your employees view you as calloused, cruel and cold.

These may seem like obvious, "no duh" statements. Use a little common sense, and it would seem clear that the best way to create positive returns is to be positive. But you have no idea how many business leaders and managers have not figured that out. Let me remind you that the only way to be truly successful in business is to ride the shoulders of other people. That's hard to do if you have beaten your people into the ground.

Besides, why would you ever want to go through the tedious and time-consuming process of hiring the right person and then constantly threaten to run them off? I don't understand it, and I certainly don't advise that management strategy. As the business owner, my primary job is to help my employees grow.

Right from the start, I teach our employees the importance of goal-setting, and I emphasize the fact that I want to help them achieve their goals. I want to help them gain some skills from working for me and build their resume. I will make a profit off of their work.

But at some point, we may part ways because our employee will outgrow our organization. I understand that. So should you. Be a professional about it when that time comes.

I encourage my employees to share their goals with me—even if their goals include outgrowing my organization. There will be times when it is in the best interest of our employee to leave our organization. I will help and encourage him to reach his professional goals—no matter where they may take him—as long as he is putting maximum effort into his role at our company.

If I do that with an employee, he will promote my business for the rest of his life, even if he goes on to another opportunity. Never burn a bridge because you may want to do business with that person down the road. And if I create the right opportunities for his growth in my company, he might end up fighting for his own dreams and my company's visions for decades. It takes tremendous effort to find the right person, so you must also put effort into keeping that person on staff. The biggest key to retaining employees probably has more to do with extending praise than a raise.

Despite what you may think, most people are not money motivated. You will discover that when you begin to administer the personality profiles. In general, most people will take less money for more security. The amount of the paycheck is not as important as the positive work environment. And if you make it a constant practice to walk through your office and compliment your employees for a job well done, you will be amazed at how productive and proactive your employees will become. This is even more important in this day and age then ever before.

The College Journal, a production of *The Wall Street Journal*, wrote an interesting story in April 2007 that documents the increasing need for praise in the workplace. Here are some excerpts from that article: "Childhood in recent decades has been defined

Performance Factors	Poor	Good	Excellent
Quality of Work	☐	☐	☑
Quantity of Work	☐	☐	☑
Dependability	☐	☑	☐
Communication Skills	☐	☐	☑
Supervision	☐	☐	☑
Leadership Skills	☐	☐	☑
Initiative	☐	☐	☐
Cooperation	☐	☐	☐
Relations	☐	☐	☐
Adaptability	☐	☐	☐
Versatility	☐	☐	☐

by stroking. By parents who see their job as building self-esteem, by soccer coaches who give every player a trophy, by schools that used to name one "student of the month" and these days name 40. Now, as this generation grows up, the culture of praise is reaching deeply into the adult world. Bosses, professors and mates are feeling the need to lavish praise on young adults, particularly twentysomethings, or else see them wither under an unfamiliar compliment deficit.

Employers are dishing out kudos to workers for little more than showing up. Corporations including Lands' End and Bank of America are hiring consultants to teach managers how to compliment employees using email, prize packages and public displays of appreciation. The 1,000-employee Scooter Store Inc., a power-wheelchair and scooter firm in New Braunfels, Texas, has a staff "celebrations assistant" whose job it is to throw confetti—25 pounds a week—at employees. She also passes out 100 to 500 celebratory helium balloons a week. The Container Store Inc. estimates that one of its 4,000 employees receives praise every 20 seconds, through such efforts as its "Celebration Voice Mailboxes."

America's praise fixation has economic, labor and social ramifications. Adults who were overpraised as children are apt to be narcissistic at work and in personal relationships, says Jean

Twenge, a psychology professor at San Diego State University. "Narcissists aren't good at basking in other people's glory, which makes for problematic marriages and work relationships", she says.

Her research suggests that young adults today are more self-centered than previous generations. For a multiuniversity study released this year, 16,475 college students took the standardized narcissistic personality inventory, responding to such statements as "I think I am a special person." Students' scores have risen steadily since the test was first offered in 1982. The average college student in 2006 was 30 percent more narcissistic than the average student in 1982.

Bob Nelson, billed as "the Guru of Thank You," counsels 80 to 100 companies a year on praise issues. He has done presentations for managers of companies such as Walt Disney Co. and Hallmark Cards Inc., explaining how different generations have different expectations. As he sees it, those over age 60 tend to like formal awards, presented publicly. But they're more laid back about needing praise, and more apt to say: "Yes, I get recognition every week. It's called a paycheck." Baby boomers, Mr. Nelson finds, often prefer being praised with more self-indulgent treats such as free massages for women and high-tech gadgets for men.

Workers under 40, he says, require far more stroking. They often like "trendy, name-brand merchandise" as rewards, but they also want near-constant feedback. "It's not enough to give praise only when they're exceptional, because for years they've been getting praise just for showing up," he says.

Mr. Nelson advises bosses: If a young worker has been chronically late for work and then starts arriving on time, commend him. "You need to recognize improvement. That might seem silly to older generations, but today, you have to do these things to get the performances you want," he says. Casey Priest, marketing vice president for Container Store, agrees. "When you set an expectation and an employee starts to meet it, absolutely praise them for it," she says."

Personally, I believe you can go overboard on the praise. But it's a trend that you must understand if you want to keep your employees happy. In fact, it's of vital importance. Now, simply praising your people is not enough to keep them motivated. You must also pay people a fair wage. Not extravagant, but fair. One of the biggest problems in Western civilized culture is something I call the "General Motors Factor." In 1965, a guy goes to work for G.M. fresh out of high school and they pay him $5,000 a year to put lug nuts on a car. In the year 2005, the guy is still standing there putting lug nuts on a car. Is he bringing any more value to GM in 2005 than he brought in 1965?

No. But he is making ridiculous amount of money now to perform the same role he did 40 years ago. That's why G.M. is going to go out of business. If you're going to work for me and you want a raise, you're going to have to bring more value to our company. Most of our employees are on some kind of incentive-based pay. They get a base salary and bonus or they're on straight commission. If they're on base salary, they get some sort of bonus quarterly based on the company's performance. Let me repeat that: The bonus is based on the company's performance, and not their own. I choose to award bonuses to our salaried employees in this manner to build a team mentality.

I've tried all different kinds of incentive packages, and that one has worked the best for me. Your salary is based on individual performance, but the bonus is a team achievement. So, if Betty sees that Billy is struggling to get his orders processed, Betty is motivated to help Billy process the orders and meet the team objectives. We normally have three or four objectives set up for the company on an annual basis. Every quarter, I cover the goals and meet with specific teams as a group. I tell them this is where we are, this is how we're doing, and here's the bonus category we scored in. It's not the same bonus payment for each person. It might be $2,000 for you because you're a $25,000 per-year employee, while I might reward $10,000 to the CFO, but the criteria for achievement is the same.

I believe the bonus structure is part of the overall motivation plan and retention because the employees must achieve the goals to receive the rewards. But there are other motivating factors, as well. Just as it is important to praise your employees, it's also important for some of them to feel part of the team through social settings, happy hours and other get-togethers. Remember those personality profiles? Some employees thrive on a happy hour or two.

My personality profile defines me as an enterpriser, and if you're reading this with the plan to open or build your own business, there's a good chance you are an enterpriser too. I don't really care about anything but the bottom line. I'm straight to the point. But remember, it takes all kinds to run a successful business. The togetherness people want a free beer and a social hour, and it's amazing how much goodwill you can spread in your office if you offer this as an option. I recently hired a marketing person and told her that it was part of her job to market the company externally and internally. I said, "You've got money to do six mixers a year." So, one of the mixers she came up with was "Hispanic Heritage Night." A half an hour after work on a Friday night, everyone came together for margaritas and nachos. The togetherness people LOVED IT. They can't wait for the next one. My salespeople, on the other hand, think it's the biggest waste of time they've ever seen. They are inspired by the paycheck; they are driven by their commissions; they are the ones actually motivated by money. But remind your salespeople—and possibly yourself—that it takes all kinds of people to run your office, and it all takes all kinds of motivation to keep people happy.

Another key to retaining employees is to offer great benefits. In fact, I have found that many people will work for less money if you provide great benefits. We provide heath insurance, a 401K plan with profit sharing, disability insurance, etc. We also provide financial planning, a credit union membership and other pieces to help people achieve their own financial goals. Most of those benefits don't cost corporations a lot of money. You just have to put them in place, and you have to sell those benefits to your employees to make sure they use them. Again, I'm selling my employees on achieving their dreams and developing themselves…and that takes constant training.

TRAINING

Training may be the most important part of the equation in developing your people and growing your company. And it's an area where most companies fail miserably. The problem with our society is that people expect to go to work, sit at a desk and make more money over time. It's the "General Motors Factor."

In my business, if you want to make more money, you've got to bring value to the company. The only way you can do that is to train—train yourself to be more effective at what you're doing now and train to learn new techniques. I don't just send my people to training seminars and classes; I go, as well. And I share that

information with my people. When I hold meetings with my sales leaders, I often request that they read professional development books that I have chosen. Perhaps less than 20 percent of them will actually do something with that information, but if I can just keep bringing them along a little bit at a time, then it's worth it. My goal is to have everyone improve a little each day.

As I have previously mentioned, there are no overnight successes, and there are no overnight millionaires. Just like a championship athletic team, it takes years of training before the team goal is reached. A coach doesn't cover the entire playbook on the first day of practice and toss it into the garbage can because he covered it all. On the contrary, he adds a play here and a play there throughout the year; he studies the tendencies of other successful programs and implements elements into his own; he is constantly teaching, developing and training. You, as a business owner or manager, should do the same… so long as you do not do it with the volatility of Mike Ditka. As far as training goes, we teach six fundamental classes over and over and over again. I make the same people sit through the classes over and over, year after year.

One of my agents recently wrote about the class. He said, "The first time I went to that class I got something out of it. Then I was told I had to be there again and I thought to myself, 'How freaking stupid is this?' But I want to thank you because I walked away from there with about ten more good things I can use in my business."

That's always my goal with training. He may forget five of those ten things next week. But when he comes back next year for another training session, he'll take the five he actually implemented last year and add another two or three things this year. Repetition in

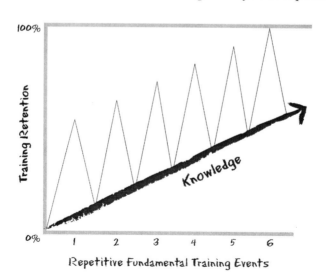

Repetitive Fundamental Training Events

training is critical. Why does a football team run the same play in practice hundreds of times a year?

Without constant practice, you are eventually going to forget the basics when the game is on the line. Likewise, the key to successful companies is training and practice. You have to sit down with people and quiz them over and over again. You have to ask them how they did that, and why they did something in a certain way. I can't teach you how to train. I can't teach you how to teach, but I can tell you that you have to do it and you have to do it over and over and over again. You can't quit. You can't ever grow tired of training. If you want to get paid like a pro, practice like one.

SAYING GOOD-BYE

The final thing I want to cover in this chapter is not necessarily a pleasant topic. You must hire people to grow your business, and— sooner or later—you must fire people to protect your business. But before we talk about firing, let's talk about laying people off. Let's say that you're building your business and things don't go the way you want so you have to lay some people off. Let's say you have $1million in payroll and your unemployment rate is 1 percent. That's what the government taxes you to pay for the unemployment pool. Unemployment is not funded by the state government; the employers fund unemployment. So they're charging you 1 percent of $1 million, which is $10,000. So $10,000 is your annual tax on that money.

Now, let's say you choose to lay off two or three people and reduce your expenses by $100,000. You laid them off so now your payroll is $900,000, but your unemployment rate went from 1 percent to 5 percent. Now, your tax rate went from $10,000 to $45,000. Did you save? No. So when you decide to make layoffs or fire someone, make sure you do it in a manner that's most advantageous to the employee and the company. If you're laying somebody off because you're out of money, you need to see your financial difficulties far enough in advance where you can help that person land on his feet somewhere else. Don't hand him a pink slip and wish him luck. Let him know that things are not going well, that he's been a great guy, and that you've got your feelers out for him. Help him look for a new job, let him use your office equipment and work time to find his new position, which can generate goodwill and save you money in the long run.

I have had to lay people off in the past when a product was pulled from me. I had to layoff 12 people. I found most of them jobs before the layoff. Laying off and firing people are both very, very difficult. You know you're hurting that person's family. But there are times when you just have to say, "You're done."

The key to firing people is to have a documented disciplinary process. It varies for each state, so make sure you review it carefully with your legal representation. Hiring, firing, motivating, aligning and training can be a tedious process with the potential for high liability exposure. Be sure to review all of your processes with attorneys, and I strongly urge you to consider purchasing employment practices liability insurance (EPLI).

I know we have covered an awful lot of information in this chapter, and it is—by far—the longest chapter in the book. But there's a good reason for that. As I have said twice previously—and as I want you to commit to memory—Your **personal** success or failure may ultimately be determined by your **personnel** success or failure.

GAME DAY PREP

1. If you truly want to grow your business and generate the lifestyle that you envision, you are ultimately going to need to invest in:
   A. Italian suits.
   B. Leather office furniture.
   C. Really cool coffee makers.
   D. People.
   Answer here_____

2. Your goal in hiring people should always be to:
   A. Hire someone who is really sexy.
   B. Hire the next superstar in your industry.
   C. Hire someone tall enough to help your corporate basketball team.
   D. Hire someone so dumb that it makes you feel really smart.
   Answer here_____

3. Once you develop a hiring process, you should:
   A. Put every potential employee through it, no matter how well you know them or how many references you have about them.
   B. Toss it out the window if your sister recommends her husband's cousin's neighbor.
   C. Constantly test it, examine it and refine it.
   D. A and C.
   Answer here_____

More detailed information about the topics covered in this chapter is available at www.gameplanbook.com.

The website is continually updated to provide the latest information, forms, instructions and tips to help you build or grow your business.

Extra Points - Notes

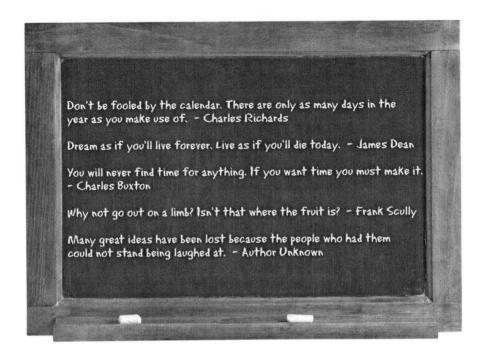

Don't be fooled by the calendar. There are only as many days in the year as you make use of. – Charles Richards

Dream as if you'll live forever. Live as if you'll die today. – James Dean

You will never find time for anything. If you want time you must make it. – Charles Buxton

Why not go out on a limb? Isn't that where the fruit is? – Frank Scully

Many great ideas have been lost because the people who had them could not stand being laughed at. – Author Unknown

CHAPTER 7

BUILD A DYNASTY

On November 3, 1948, the *Chicago Daily Tribune* printed one of the most famously erroneous headlines in United States history: "Dewey Defeats Truman." You have undoubtedly seen the picture of a smiling President Harry S. Truman holding up that front-page newspaper headline as he celebrated being elected to his second term in the White House. That moment still ranks as one of the all-time gaffes in media memoirs. And even today, it should serve as a reminder to all of us that you should NOT always believe what the front page of the newspaper is telling you. Not then. Not now. Not ever.

Way back in the opening of this book, I warned you not to pay attention to the naysayers who will inevitably take their shots at you as you open a business or expand your organization. That could be a negative neighbor; it could be a brooding brother; or it could be a calloused co-worker. But the negativity will not only come from people that you know. It will also come from the news media. If you want to build a business, believe in your dreams, believe in yourself and believe in your future. But do not necessarily believe the media. No matter how emphatically the reporter writes it; no matter how boldly the editorial headline writer states it; no matter how forcefully the television news anchorman says it; and no matter how many reputable Internet sites may report it, let me strongly encourage you not to blindly buy into everything that the media are trying to sell you.

Think about it this way: Most newspapers are sold at a price range from .25 cents to about $1.50. In life, you typically get what you pay for. If you spend $10 on a pair of sunglasses, do you expect impeccable quality and lifetime durability? If you spend $3 on lunch, do you expect five-star service?

Of course not. But for some reason, many of us expect reliable, high-quality, unbiased and valuable information from a newspaper that costs us a couple of quarters. Now, I'm not suggesting that you should give up your newspaper subscription. Keep buying the papers if you like and read all of the information that the media provides you. Listen to it, ponder it, discuss it, deliberate it and—by all means—use it to your advantage. But especially in terms of how it applies to your business plans, procedures and goals, remember that what was true some 60 years ago—probably even 600 years ago, for that matter—is also true today: The media can often be quite misleading. As Mark Twain once said: "If you don't read the newspaper, you are uninformed. If you do read the newspaper, you are misinformed."

Before I continue any further mauling of the media, I want to point out that the point of this chapter is not to bash the media (although I must admit that it is a lot of fun). And actually, I must confess that I do believe there are many good journalists...at least on ESPN's *SportsCenter.* But unless you are tuning in to ESPN for the latest score, I caution you to be careful. What you hear is not always completely factual; what you read is not always straightforward; and what you believe from the media should be carefully considered and calculated.

I have no idea what day it is as you are reading this. I cannot possibly foretell the stock market of the future or the economic indicators of today. But I am willing to bet that if you pick up today's newspaper that you will find plenty of gloomy financial forecasts for tomorrow. Go ahead, try it. Skim the headlines on the front page, the regional section or the financial/business section. Chances are that you would find enough negativity to be quite discouraged about starting or expanding your business. I base this assumption on the fact that the newspaper industry—and probably all media outlets, for that matter—loves to predict pitfalls, not windfalls. If you are waiting for the media to tell you that the time is right to expand your business, you might as well wait for Barry Bonds to voluntarily have his name removed from the home run record because of steroid use.

Don't hold your breath. It's probably not going to happen, so quit waiting. If you pick up the newspaper every morning and scan the headlines, you will inevitably be convinced that entrepreneurship is a dead end road. You will read words like "recession, inflation, unemployment, budget deficit, trade deficit, falling housing rates, rising gas prices, escalating interest rates, and bankruptcy." It's enough to depress even the most optimistic entrepreneur. But remember this: "Dewey Defeats Truman."

Here's the reality: The media does not favor entrepreneurs. Not every reporter hates every successful businessman. And every editor is certainly not envious of every capitalist. But you would be absolutely amazed at how envious most journalists are of entrepreneurs. And you would be shocked if you fully understood how left of center the media really are. I realize

that liberal bias in the media is a tiresome subject. We have been hearing about it for at least 30 years. But I believe this is a very important subject to cover in an entrepreneurial book because understanding the depth of that bias can change the way you think, the way you interpret the news, the direction of your business and your day-to-day decisions.

Remember to never take advice from someone who doesn't have what you want. If you are looking for advice from a newspaper columnist or story, carefully consider the source. If you are tempted not to make an acquisition, not to merge or not to expand because of the gloomy economic articles you keep reading, remember that the writer is probably paying his electricity bill with a VISA and his grocery bill with a MasterCard. It's difficult to be optimistic about the economy when you can't even pay your own bills.

The other thing to remember with the media—print and electronic—is that journalists tend to paint a gloomier scenario when it may benefit or support their own personal situation or belief. Study after study—including a very interesting one by Tim Groseclose of UCLA and Jeff Milyo of the University of Chicago—have shown that the liberal media tend to be more negative about the economy when a Republican is in the White House. In an analysis of the study, the Pew Research Center wrote: "Groseclose and Milyo also examined at the political orientation of journalists relative to the population. They noted that just seven percent of journalists voted for George H.W. Bush in 1992 versus 37 percent of the voting public. In other words, journalists are more liberal than voters in even the most liberal congressional district in the United States, the ninth district in California, which contains the city of Berkeley. Even there, Bush received 12 percent of the vote, almost twice his support among journalists."

I could go on and on about how anti-entrepreneurial the media are. I have a suitcase full of citations, studies and examples that would expose the misrepresentations. I refer to all of this media misrepresentation as "Chicken Little" journalism. In fact, I recently had a two-day meeting with my sales staff entitled "Chicken Little." Several of my salespeople had obviously been reading too many newspapers and watching too much television. They were buying the "economy is turning down" B.S. that the media were feeding them. And some of the members of my sales staff were beginning to believe that the "sky is falling." It's not, and all you have to do to realize that is to drive through the parking lot of your local grocery store. Look around the lot. How many 'junkers' do you see? How many jalopies? How many rusted-out, dented-up lemons can you find? In your typical suburban neighborhood, you probably won't find many. And I guarantee you that there are more new cars on the road today than there were 10 or

20 years ago. Heck, for that matter, take a drive through your local high school parking lot. Generally speaking, the students today are driving much nicer vehicles than I could have ever imagined when I was in high school. Why? Because their parents, for the most part, are doing much better financially than their grandparents and great-grandparents. Yet, the economy is in the tank? Whatever.

Do you remember how Hurricane Katrina, Hurricane Rita and Hurricane Ike were going to drive gas prices up to $15 a gallon and plummet the Western civilization into economic chaos? If you read the newspapers, you were led to believe that everybody was going to dump their SUV for a micro or mini car.

But on your way to work tomorrow, look around the interstate and highways. See any shiny, new SUVs out there? Of course you do. And do you remember how the Y2K glitch was probably going to plunge our economy into the depths of hell? Or the terrorists attacks of September 11, 2001?

The economy is not in the tank—and it's not heading for third-world status—just because the media are saying it is. Late in 2007, I did a little research on the home market—known in media circles as the "housing crisis"—because everyone seemed to be claiming that it was falling apart. What I found is that there were 100 percent more homes being sold in Houston in 2007 than there were in 1993. The new home starts, or housing permits, had doubled. But you probably won't read about those numbers in the local newspaper. The sky isn't falling, and even if the Dow drops, it's probably going to come back up again. And make sure you understand this: If your business stalls; if your profits dwindle; if your customers decrease; or if your worries increase, it's time to expand. Do not hunker down in a bunker mentality. Do not panic. Do not dramatically slash prices and cut employees. And DO NOT blame the economy. Grow. Build. Diversify. Take a leap of faith.

RECESSION-PROOF YOUR BUSINESS

The last really good story I read about the financial woes of our economy was *The Grapes of Wrath* by John Steinbeck, which was published in 1939. That's a fictional novel set during the Great Depression. For the most part, reporters and broadcasters have been mimicking Steinbeck ever since, writing loosely-based fictional pieces about the status of the economy. But for the sake of argument, let's say that a recession is eventually coming. How do you guard yourself against it? The same way you reach your goals in a booming economy: You act aggressively. You expand your revenue sources. You grow your business.

Many of us start out in business with a narrow-minded focus. We want to do one thing well, and we spend an enormous amount of time focusing on doing that one thing well. That's not necessarily a bad way to start a business. But it's a recipe for disaster over

the long haul. You must constantly examine your business structure and consider ways to diversify your product line and your revenue streams. And I encourage you not to wait until the perceived time is right. If you wait for the economists to tell you that the time is right; if you wait for your profits to reach a certain level; and if you wait until the media say it's time to expand, you will likely miss the boat altogether. It's the same principle as having children. If we all waited until our married lives, our finances, our houses were perfectly in order before we started having children, the human race would be extinct by now. Sometimes you must simply go for it and work out the details on the fly. This is especially true when diversifying your product line.

For the sake of example, let's say that you sell or manufacture scissors. You may have the best scissors in the country, and you may have made your reputation on scissors. But if you are only selling scissors, you're probably going to be in trouble at some point in the future. You need to be looking to diversify your product line and make knives. Or office supplies. Or razor blades. Or box cutters. Or all of the above.

If you're in the insurance business, you may have started with auto insurance. And, while you may be really good at selling auto coverage, you need to expand into multiple product lines to be successful. You need to expand into homes, small commercial, large commercial, health and life insurance to protect yourself from the inevitable dips and valleys that will come your way. What should drive your focus—no matter what your industry or specialty has previously been—is the potential revenue you can earn per customer. The more revenue you can generate from one client, the better off you are. And the more likely you are to retain that customer.

That's the recipe for so many business success stories. Case in point: Wal-Mart. For the fiscal year that ended January, 31, 2006, Wal-Mart generated more than $312.4 billion in global revenue. And according to the company's website in January of 2008, Sam Walton's original general store concept—which began with a single store in Rogers, Arkansas in 1962—includes more than 1.9 million associates worldwide and nearly 7,000 stores and wholesale clubs across 14 countries.

"The secret of successful retailing is to give your customers what they want," Sam Walton wrote in his autobiography. "And really, if you think about it from the point of view of the customer, you want everything: a wide assortment of good quality merchandise; the lowest possible prices; guaranteed satisfaction with what you buy; friendly, knowledgeable service; convenient hours; free parking; a pleasant shopping experience. You love it when you visit a store that somehow exceeds your expectations, and you hate it when a store inconveniences you, or gives you a hard time, or pretends you're invisible."

That sounds like a great business philosophy, doesn't it? But with respect to the late Sam Walton, let's be honest. Do you know anybody who actually enjoys shopping at Wal-Mart? Did you receive friendly, knowledgeable service the last time you went into Wal-Mart? Did your experience at Wal-Mart exceed your expectations?

The answers to those questions are likely, no, no and no. It's quite easy to feel invisible at Wal-Mart. Yet, Wal-Mart continues to thrive. According to the company website, net sales for the third quarter of fiscal year 2008 were approximately $90.9 billion, an increase of 8.8 percent over the record-setting third quarter of fiscal year 2007. The secret isn't great service. It's the diversity of goods. It's the convenience of one-stop shopping. Wal-Mart was doing exceptionally well in the early and mid-1980s, but the company truly took off in the late 1980s. Why? Wal-Mart added more goods, as the first Supercenter, featuring a complete grocery department along with the 36 departments of general merchandise, opened in 1988. The company has been soaring ever since. Of course, the other side of Wal-Mart's phenomenal success is that its growth and expansions have resulted in hundreds of thousands of mom and pop grocery stores, hardware stores, general stores, paint stores, etc. going out of business.

The lesson to be learned here is this: Your scissors may be cutting edge, but your competition will eventually slice you to pieces if you do not expand your product line. Your customers will simply not keep coming back if all you offer them is scissors—no matter how sharp you are.

Here's a real-world example from my business: Policy retention in the insurance industry is essentially the same thing as customer retention in any other business. In our business, the deeper you are in the household, the more likely it is to keep your customers. If I have ten customers and those ten customers bought one auto policy from me, in ten years, I'd retain one of those customers. With just one auto policy, it would be quite

easy for those customers to shop around for the best price and to leave me for another provider on a whim. But statistics show that if I had sold them two lines of business—let's say home and auto insurance—after ten years I'd have seven customers or 70 percent retention. And if I had sold three lines—let's say home, auto and life—then I'd likely retain nine of those ten customers over the span of a decade. People aren't likely to leave because it's a hassle to change three policies or more. For the average consumer, if you're two or three lines deep, you're pretty much golden with them. So one of your strategies as an insurance business owner is to get multiple policies with that customer. But it's not just applicable to the insurance industry. The lesson applies to virtually every business.

Think about the fast food industry. Let's use the king of all fast food, McDonald's, as the example. Back in 1954, 52 year-old Ray Kroc mortgaged his home and invested his entire life savings to become the exclusive distributor of a five-spindled milk shake maker called the Multimixer. Not long afterward, Kroc heard about a McDonald's hamburger stand in California running eight Multimixers at a time. So, he packed up his car and headed West to see the operation with his own eyes. According to the McDonald's Corporation website, Kroc had never seen so many people served so quickly when he pulled up to take a look. He then pitched the idea of opening up several restaurants to the brothers Dick and Mac McDonald, convinced that he could sell eight of his Multimixers to each and every one.

Key point to remember here: Kroc was not initially interested in becoming the king of fast food. He was initially focused on selling his Multimixers. But seeing the opportunity to combine his Multimixers with the McDonald brothers' hamburgers, Kroc opened the first McDonald's in Des Plaines, Illinois in 1955. The first day's revenues were a whopping $366.12.

Originally, it was all about hamburgers, French fries and milkshakes. But in 1963, the happy clown, Ronald McDonald, made his first

TV appearance. The not-so-subtle suggestion was that going to McDonald's was as much fun as going to the circus. And kids across America took notice. In 1968, the Big Mac® was introduced to further expand the menu and brand the corporation, and in 1973, the company took a huge leap of faith when it introduced the Egg McMuffin®. No longer was McDonald's simply a place to grab a quick lunch or an inexpensive dinner; it was now serving breakfast. Expanding. Diversifying. Growing.

I think it's also important to point out here that 1973 was considered to be one of the worst economic years in the United States in the post-World War II era. That was the year when the members of the Organization of Arab Petroleum Exporting Countries (OAPEC, consisting of the Arab members of OPEC plus Egypt and Syria) announced, as a result of the ongoing Yom Kippur War, that they would no longer ship oil to nations that had supported Israel in its conflict with Syria and Egypt. And on November 26, 1973, *TIME* Magazine wrote the following: "Even before the Arabs' oil embargo, forecasters almost unanimously predicted a slowdown for the U.S. economy next year. Now fears are growing that the oil crisis could lead the nation closer to a recession, with some rises in unemployment, heightened inflation and widespread shortages of vital petroleum-based products."

TIME, along with many other media outlets, predicted inflation, a decline in the gross national product, recession and gloom. In hindsight, the economists were correct: The GNP declined from 1973 to 1975, as inflation and the unemployment rate increased along with the lines at the gas pumps. Conventional business wisdom during such a time might be to hold your ground and survive the recession. But Kroc expanded his product line. And the results were phenomenal. He did it again in 1979, when McDonald's introduced the Happy Meal®. Now, every fast food chain has some kind of kids meal with a toy inside. And in more recent years, the company has answered the call of more health conscious consumers with grilled chicken wraps, salads and even a gourmet coffee line to compete with Starbucks.

CORE BUSINESS

Imagine what McDonald's would be today if Kroc would have simply been content with selling decent burgers, good milkshakes and outstanding french fries. He could have hung his hat on those french fries or simply made a few bucks on his Multimixers. But he expanded—even during the most trying financial times—and built a global empire as a result. Now, mom and dad can get a healthy salad at McDonald's while the kids eat Chicken McNuggets® in their Happy Meals® and the grandparents sip gourmet coffee over ice cream. McDonald's may still be famous for its french fries, but it has capitalized on producing multiple revenue streams.

I believe you must always focus on your core business, but it is important to go into business thinking about expansion and diversification. And those thoughts never need to be pushed to the backburner. As soon as you slow down, your competition will catch up. If you open up a yard business, I think you need to be constantly striving toward also opening a pool service and perhaps a Christmas lights service. If you are already going to be on location to mow the yard, why not take care of the pool, as well? And when the grass stops growing, why not offer your customers professional Christmas lights installation and removal? Maybe you could also consider expanding into insect and pest control. If you are into that house for four lines of service—as opposed to one—you have a much greater chance of retaining the customer when the cute kid from across the street offers to mow the lawn for a much cheaper rate.

MORE STORES

Expanding your product or service line is a key component to retaining your customers and growing your business in the best or bleakest of financial times. So, too, is expanding your store locations.

One of the most proven and time-tested methods of growing your business is expanding your number of locations. It's the divide and conquer method that chains have been implementing for decades. And from personal experience I can tell you that duplicating your efforts in secondary locations is much easier than starting up your first storefront. You learn plenty of valuable lessons in opening your first storefront; you learn what to do; and you understand what not to do. But let me warn you about opening that second storefront: Don't plan for just one other location. Plan for multiple ones.

There's an old story I learned in distribution that applies to virtually every business and industry that I have studied or encountered. Simply put, if you want to do business with a plumber, do it with a plumber who has one truck or at least three. Never do business with a plumber who has two trucks. If he has one truck, he's probably a really good plumber because he knows everything that is going on in his business. But if he has only two trucks, beware of doing business with him because he may know what's happening in his truck, but he is probably not aware of what is happening with the other truck. I can't really explain this scientifically. But I truly believe that when you go from owning one store to two stores, you typically try to do and oversee everything that happens at both stores, which is impossible to do. Your attention is so divided between the two stores that you lose your focus, and things begin to slip through the cracks. I've seen this happen to hundreds of businesses and business owners through the years. Store No. 2 can often be disastrous. But when you open up the third store or roll out the third truck, something typically happens that makes you realize you can no longer oversee every detail; you can no longer have your hands in every decision and every move the company makes. The third store forces you to go into a managerial role, where you make big-picture decisions and serve as the leader of the company instead of the jack-of-all-trades of the organization.

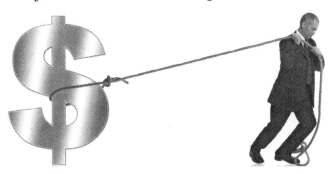

This is an essential step in the evolution of a leader. You don't have to open up multiple locations to take this step. As I have mentioned previously, I encourage you to draw out your organizational chart long before you have the money or manpower to fill in that chart with actual employees. But if your dream scenario includes multiple locations, I strongly advise you to plan on opening at least two additional locations—not including your original storefront. If you simply open one more store, statistics prove that it will be very difficult for you to succeed. Force yourself to think big. Once you have three locations, you have moved into another realm of ownership and entrepreneurship. And the key to success at that level is keeping the big picture in mind and keeping the right people in place (go back and review the last chapter about recruiting and retaining top employees, if necessary).

Another way your business can grow is through mergers and acquisitions. Those seem to be scary words to many small business owners, but I assure you that the process is not scary at all, and it can be very profitable. You can sometimes find businesses for pennies on the dollar. And in the process, you can help out a desperate business owner while turning a significant profit for yourself. I am constantly searching websites for businesses for sale, and about once a month I will go out and look at some of the most interesting businesses that I have seen on the net. As I write today, I am currently in the middle of a $9 million acquisition with an insurance agency. It may happen and it may not. In all of my negotiations, I believe it should be a good deal for both parties. In this case, he is looking to move into financial planning, and I am looking to expand my operations. The key to any acquisition or merger is to make certain it is a good fit for you and it works into your plans. I've seen some people purchase a business just to say they have bought a business. That's not necessarily a good strategy. You want to first make certain that the business you are considering will be more of a gain than a financial strain.

Is it currently successful? Does it have the potential to be more successful? Does adding this location strengthen the core of my company? How quickly can I turn it around for a profit? Do I want to keep this business for the long-term? Will the current owner stay on as a consultant?

These are all questions you must ask yourself in the preliminary stages of purchasing a business. Let's look at the acquisition that I previously mentioned. I want to walk you through the thought processes of the deal. It made good financial sense for me, and the owner wanted to go into another line of work. He agreed—along with a couple of other family members/ employees—to stay on as consultants so the clients that are used to them can deal with them in the initial phases of the transition. The current owners agreed to sign employment contracts because we want their names to still be associated with the agency. We then structured a deal to pay $400,000 up front, and the payout is variable based on the revenue the business generates. We'll pay them about $250,000 a year for three years and then—if the business is a certain size at the end of the third year—we'll pay them a $300,000 bonus. So

we're going to buy the business for probably $1 million, and it is variable based on its performance. There may be a million different ways to structure a deal like this, and this one could change four or five times if the acquisition goes through.

The point here is that I would never go write a check for a restaurant or anything and simply take the business. You always want to incorporate terms in the contract from the current ownership so that they will help you be successful. Imagine how much different the automotive sales business would be if the salesperson who was selling the car had to carry the note. He would likely be real honest about what was going on with that car if he knew it was coming back to him broken and you didn't have to

OPPORTUNITIES

make any more payments. You can essentially do that through the terms of your acquisition contract. With the acquisition, we would make the owner sign a consulting agreement so he won't go out and say negative things about our business, and you can also enforce a non-compete clause so that he won't pirate your customers. There are a number of things you can do to help ensure the success of the business when making the acquisition. Just make sure to involve your legal representation in the acquisition at every stage of the negotiations. And make sure the acquisition makes financial sense to you.

When you begin looking for opportunities, some will come along that will just not make financial sense. Some very small insurance agents have contacted me in the past about buying their operations. Occasionally, I've done it simply to gain the desks, furniture, assets, etc. But more often than not, I have passed on small agencies because they simply do not fit into my master plans. But they may be a good acquisition for someone just beginning. So, be careful before you move on an acquisition, but DO NOT be afraid to begin looking. As long as you have your lawyer with you, it can be a very beneficial arrangement.

Mergers can also help you grow your business in some situations. You see it happen all the time in the field of law, and I have seen numerous examples of it working well in the insurance industry. If you're really good at commercial insurance services, and I'm a pro at home and auto insurance, we might be better off in the long haul by merging our two talents and our staffs and going forward. This can be an exceptional way to attract new business to your organization, but it also means that you are now partners with someone else. Make sure you know that partner; make sure you have similar goals and ambitions; and make certain you involve your legal representation in the merger. Handshakes are great for introductions, but they are not adequate when it comes to making business deals.

Protect yourself; protect your assets; protect everything by involving legal representation before agreeing to anything. You need to decide what is fair and best for both parties in the initial negotiations, and include everything in the contract so that if the deal goes south neither party should be upset because they agreed to the terms of the contract. In other words, decide how to end your relationship in the begining...while you are still friends.

BE READY TO ADAPT, CHANGE AND EVOLVE

As your business grows, you must constantly be on the lookout for ways to improve your operations, generate more sales, add new employees, increase your revenue streams, diversify your products or services, utilize emerging technologies and keep track of a myriad of responsibilities and opportunities. But as you evaluate your office operations, don't forget to take a look in the mirror. As your company grows, your role is not the only thing that needs to change. You may also need to change your business structure, beginning at the top. I'm not just referring to a change in title; I'm talking about the way your business is structured from a legal standpoint.

When you start a business on your own, you are usually the CEO, the CFO and the TCO (toilet cleaning officer). As we have discussed previously, you often must be willing to perform every role in the office—from talking to clients to taking out the trash— to get the business going. But as your profits begin to improve and your organizational chart takes shape with the addition of employees to fill in the roles you previously performed, you need to take a look at how your business is structured.

Most small business owners are sole proprietors. They go out and file a DBA (Doing Business As) certificate with the county court house, and they start doing business in that name. It's the quickest and easiest way to open a business, but there are a couple of potential problems with that setup. First and foremost—according to the attorneys and accountants who I have consulted with—is that you're personally liable for all of the mistakes that your company makes. Let's say your company is called Joe's Accounting. If you set up the company as an entity (such as a corporation, limited partnership or limited liability company) where it has its own social security number, which is called an EIN (Employer Identification Number), if a mistake is made, clients can sue Joe's Accounting but they can't sue Joe for his personal assets. But if you set it up as a sole proprietorship, the client can sue you, Joe—and not just Joe's Accounting.

If you're going to operate as an entity as opposed to being a sole proprietor, you must document and follow the corporate or partnership rules for performing as an entity. If you're the president of Joe's Accounting, you need to sign things "Joe Owner, President." If you sign everything "Joe Owner" the corporate veil you are operating under can be pierced in court, and clients can come after you individually because you weren't really acting as a corporation; it was just a front. I've seen many business owners who will incorporate, but will keep on doing business the same way they did business when they were a sole proprietor.

CORPORATION

Here's an example: If you're a corporation and you want to buy something of any significant value you need to have a resolution signed that says something like, "The Board of Directors of Joe's Accounting allows Joe Owner to purchase a new Cadillac Escalade." You sign that resolution and you put it in your minutes book. The Board of Directors can be you, or you and your wife, in a small corporation. You can be every position in the corporation. But you need to document those things and

have that transactional history so that if someone were to ever sue you, you can prove that you were acting as a corporation, not a sole proprietorship. Most good attorneys will help you with your corporate minutes and make sure you're doing things correctly. So, make sure—as we have discussed previously—to have legal representation and a good accountant. And use them both whenever a question or concern arises.

I started out as a sole proprietor. My reasons weren't liability because I had plenty of insurance to protect me from any lawsuit. The reason I changed that setup was because my accountant called me one day and said, 'Do you know that 25 percent of all sole proprietors with more than $200,000 on their tax return are audited?' I had no idea, but I also knew that I did not want to go through the headaches and time constraints of being audited.

So, I decided to switch from a sole proprietorship to a corporation because, quite frankly, not many of them are audited. There are so many corporations with revenues much larger than mine, so I am considered a small fish in a big pond, which is actually a huge advantage when it comes to IRS scrutiny. Today our entity is even more complex. Our main company is a limited partnership between the Warren E. Barhorst Agency and Barhorst Management Group. They partner together for tax and liability reasons. I also own a partnership in the company that wrote this book. There are a number of legitimate reasons for setting up corporate structures, partnerships and LLCs. I won't bore you with all the details here, but I strongly encourage you to sit down with your board, which includes your peers, your attorney, your accountant and your banker, to determine what makes the most sense in your situation. And your situation today may be much different than what it is a year from now.

So, schedule regular meetings with your board. It's worth the cost. Many small business owners don't understand the complexities of how their own business is set up. They miss tax advantages and—much worse—find themselves in a world of trouble because they'll buy into something and then they end up getting sued. A prudent businessman incorporates or forms another entity besides himself. So, explore the best possibilities and options for your own situation.

A FINAL WORD BEFORE YOU TACKLE THE WORLD

I want to finish with the same words I used to begin this book: "You've got what it takes." I truly believe that virtually every one of us on this planet is capable of achieving great things—far greater than most us ever actually accomplish. But what separates our realities from our potential prosperity is often simply a lack of confidence. Far too many people settle for an average job, an average income and an average life because they are afraid to step out on their own and take a risk.

Please do not be afraid to take the risk that you are considering. Only with risk do you find true reward in life. Take a leap of faith; set your goals, do things the right way; treat people as you would like to be treated; work your butt off and never lose sight of your dreams. You will be amazed at what you can accomplish. You've got what it takes. Believe that with all your heart. You were not put on this planet to be ordinary; you have an extraordinary purpose, but you must take a leap of faith to discover that purpose.

And now that you have completed this book, I believe that you are equipped with everything you need to start or expand your business dreams. I hope you refer to this book—and our website, www.gameplanbook.com—over and over again as you embark on the journey toward achieving your business dreams. But most of all, I hope that you don't close this book now and never return to the possibilities that your future could hold. There's a reason you picked up this book, and there's a reason that God placed the dreams you have been pondering in your heart. Act on them. The principles, plans and lessons in this book have been tested and proven successful in real-life, real-world business situations over and over again. If you learn them, follow them and adapt them to your own business, you can achieve your dreams. And if you teach your employees to do the same, you can realize dreams that you probably never even imagined to be possible.

I hope you have found this book to be entertaining; I hope it's been helpful; and I hope it has planted seeds of success. As any gardener knows, seeds usually don't grow on their own. It takes some nurturing, some fertilizing, some watering and some weed pulling to ensure that those seeds blossom into a harvest. The decisions you make and the actions you take today will determine your financial harvest of the future. Take action, stand firm in the face of adversity and believe that the seeds that have been planted will deliver you your field of dreams.

You've got what it takes.

GAME DAY PREP

1. When media members—print or electronic—tell you that the economy is in the tank, you should:
   A. Build your own bomb shelter in the backyard, stock it with supplies and get ready for all hell to break loose.
   B. Put your business up for sale and take pennies on the dollar for it if any fool is stupid enough to expand in difficult economic times.
   C. Credit Nostrodamus for predicting all this crap would happen a long time ago.
   D. Stay the course, keep the faith and look for ways to expand your business.
   Answer here _____

2. According to some of the great entrepreneurs of our time (Sam Walton, Ray Kroc, etc.) one of the keys to recession-proofing your business is:
   A. Expanding.
   B. Diversifying.
   C. Growing.
   D. All of the above.
   Answer here _____

3. Mergers and acquisitions should:
   A. Scare the ever livin' hell out of you.
   B. Be viewed as a potential way to grow and expand your business.
   C. Be handled with handshake agreements.
   D. Never involve your accountants, legal counsel or business partners.
   Answer here _____

More detailed information about the topics covered in this chapter is available at www.gameplanbook.com.

The website is continually updated to provide the latest information, forms, instructions and tips to help you build or grow your business.

Extra Points - Notes

About the Authors

Warren Barhorst is the CEO of the Barhorst Insurance Group (BIG), a Texas-based insurance and financial services firm with more than 30 offices across the state. Barhorst, a graduate of Texas A&M and a former football letterman with the Aggies, opened his first insurance office in Northwest Houston in 1993 with major dreams and minimal capital. Barhorst's entrepreneurial spirit, people skills and business vision have enabled BIG to continually expand its business scope and bottom-line profits. BIG, the No. 1 Nationwide Insurance agency in the United States was named to the *Houston Business Journal's* Fast 100 in 2008 and the 2008 *Inc.* 5,000 list. BIG was also ranked No. 3 by *Texas Monthly* on the 2008 mid-sized Best Companies to Work for in Texas list. Barhorst has earned numerous awards through the years, including the 2008 Houston and Gulf Coast area Ernst & Young Entrepreneur Of The Year.® Barhorst and his wife, Lisa, have three children—son, Spencer, and daughters, Ashley and Shelby.

Rusty Burson is currently the associate editor of *12th Man Magazine* and Vice President with the 12th Man Foundation. Burson, a 1990 graduate of Sam Houston State, began his professional career as a newspaper reporter and editor in Galveston and later in Fort Worth. After leaving the newspaper industry, Burson took a role in municipal public relations and then became an editor for numerous business publications in the Dallas-Fort Worth area. Burson joined the 12th Man Foundation, the fund-raising organization for Texas A&M athletics, in 1998. He lives in College Station with his wife, Vannessa, and the couple's three children—son, Payton, and daughters, Kyleigh and Summer. Burson has authored four previous books.